Teach Yourself®

Make Money from Freelance Writing

Claire Gillman

Hodder Education

338 Euston Road, London NW1 3BH

Hodder Education is an Hachette UK company.

First published in UK 2012 by Hodder Education

First published in US 2012 by The McGraw-Hill Companies, Inc.

Copyright © 2012 Claire Gillman

London Borough of Richmond Upon Thames		
CA		
90710 000 109 089		
Askews & Holts		
808.02 GIL		£12.99
		9781444174526

www.hoddereducation.co.uk

Cover image © Africa Studio - Fotolia

Typeset by Cenveo Publisher Services

Printed and bound by CPI Group (UK) Ltd, Croydon, CR0 4YY

Also available
in ebook

Acknowledgements

My thanks go to my agent and friend, Chelsey Fox, of Fox &
Howard, and to my publishers Sam Richardson and Sarah
Stubbs at Hodder for their support and enthusiasm during this
project. And to my husband and sons, Nick, Alex and George,
who understand and fully support me in the strange activities
and odd working hours that my freelance writer's lifestyle
sometimes demands.

Contents

Why write for a living?

In this chapter you will learn:

▶ *About the aptitudes and qualities you will need to sustain a career as a freelance writer*

▶ *About the current climate for freelance writers – both the opportunities provided by the expansion of new media and the pressures imposed by the economic downturn*

▶ *About the wide range of media outlets – from traditional media like newspapers and books to ezines and blogs – that can provide opportunities for the freelance writer.*

The traditional image of the impecunious writer scribbling away in a garret flat to earn a crust has changed significantly. Now, being a professional writer is one of the most desirable jobs available and a 2011 survey showed that the fourth most popular choice among media job hunters was to be self-employed (behind Google, the BBC and the *Guardian*).

What is it then that is so appealing about being a freelance writer? On investigation, it seems that what first attracts the uninitiated to freelance writing is not the same as the major benefits cited by many of those already in the profession.

Perhaps surprisingly, full-time freelance writers say that one of the things they value most about writing is that it offers an interesting life. As a writer, you have access to people that, in the normal course of events, you might never meet, and you experience things that you might never normally get to try. That's because, to make copy newsworthy, entertaining or informative, the topic you are writing about has to be interesting. Therefore, it stands to reason that you will be exposed to fascinating and out-of-the-ordinary people, activities, places and events because these are the fundamental ingredients of the copy that editors, publishers, producers and readers want to buy.

Remember this: Freelance writing improves your life–work balance

As a freelance writer, your life–work balance tends to be good because you can make sure you are on hand for those life events that matter to you. You never have to miss a school play, children's sports day or important anniversary or birthday again because you can always work early mornings or evenings to fit around the event.

Yet, all the many attractions of being a freelance writer amount to a hill of beans if one element is missing. Writing has to be a *pleasure* if you are to make a career of it. If you like the idea of working from home but actually find writing a bit of a chore, or you simply see it as a way of making money, then, let's be clear, there are much better ways to make a living that will pay you more without the isolation, rejections, insecurity and lack of appreciation that you get with a writing career. Yet, if writing is a joy for you, whether it's fiction, journalism, blogging or broadcasting, then there really is no finer way to be self-employed.

Writing professionally can be a liberating experience. You are able to specialize in the areas that interest you, you can change direction and specialism whenever you want, you can work anywhere in the country (or the world for that matter), and you can work the hours that suit you (deadlines notwithstanding).

That, of course, is the up-side of the career once you are established. Yet, it would be irresponsible to raise your expectations unrealistically – it's true to say that becoming a successful freelance writer is not easy, and you are unlikely to get rich in the process. But it is not impossible.

Like all things, if you want to make a decent living at it, you must apply yourself fairly studiously to your writing, and you must also master all the other aspects of being a self-employed one-man band, which means you must be able to pitch your ideas, make the sums work, chase payments and market yourself and your product. In truth, if you consider yourself an 'artiste' and are only interested in the noble art of writing itself, you would be best advised to continue writing as a hobby and a pleasure, and to earn your living in some other way.

If you are prepared to roll up your sleeves and get stuck in, to be versatile and open to investigating every potential avenue, then professional writing is a career well worth pursuing. So let's explore some of the searching questions that a writer needs to ask him/herself before giving up the day job and launching a writing career.

Key idea: Fame, if not fortune

Perhaps this should not be a prime motivator for choosing a career as a freelance writer but it has to be said that seeing your name in print is a thrill that never diminishes. I defy any writer to say that a by-line in a newspaper, blog or magazine or seeing your book on the shelf is not a huge ego-boost.

Are you suited to it?

First and foremost, you have to ask yourself whether you can write. A silly question you may think, but writing is a skill that you craft and hone over time. It is not an ability that everyone possesses. Now is the time to be candid about your aptitude. You may get great pleasure from writing but is the finished product saleable? Does it do what you set out to achieve, that is to inform, entertain or uplift the reader?

In reality, you may not be the best judge of this – and neither are your loved ones and friends, who will not be able to give unbiased feedback for fear of hurting your feelings. The best way to judge your talent is to pitch it in the commercial arena against other professional writers or to invite feedback from impartial and truthful friends/colleagues who have your best interests at heart and, preferably, some publishing experience.

Once you have established that you have the necessary writing ability, there are other qualities that are essential to the freelance writer and other obstacles to face:

SOLITUDE

Each of us needs time and space to get in touch with our creativity and to let the writing flow, but, although it can be a wonderful, absorbing and fulfilling career, writing can also be quite an isolating experience. You will spend a good deal of your time alone with your thoughts and your computer. For some, the solitude is a rare luxury. For others, it is one of the hardest aspects of writing as a career.

If you find spending large periods of time on your own difficult to handle, then you might want to reconsider whether you are cut out for writing as a full-time job. Most freelance writers who work from home will tell you that it is a double-edged sword. Advances in communications allow an author to live anywhere – all you need is a laptop and access to a telephone line and/or a postal service. Certainly, the short commute and the flexibility of being your own boss cannot be underestimated, but still working on your own as a one-man band can be a lonely career.

SELF-DISCIPLINE

You must also have the self-discipline to work at home and ignore all the distractions and temptations on offer. This is not a holiday. If you don't work, you don't get paid. Nonetheless, there are plenty of writers who fail because they fall prey to the many time-consuming distractions that eat into the working day, leaving themselves without enough time to get the work done.

FACING REJECTION

Have you got a thick skin? As a freelance writer, you will face rejection on countless occasions. It happens to the best writers and it is an occupational hazard. If you are a delicate flower who cannot stand criticism of your ideas or your work, then this is clearly not a good profession for you. And coupled with the ability to bear rejection is the need to be tenacious. If J.K. Rowling had fallen at the first fence, the world would never have witnessed the delights of the Harry Potter series. So gritting your teeth after a knock-back and persevering is another essential characteristic of the freelancer.

UNSHAKEABLE

Do you think you will be able to deal with the instability and unpredictability of being a freelance writer? Not everyone has the temperament to handle not knowing where and when the next paying project is coming from. Even for seasoned freelancers, it can be a temptation to take every piece of work offered, no matter how busy you are, as you never know when the next job will arrive. For novice writers, this 'feast or famine' scenario is an absolute reality and one you must be prepared for.

INQUISITIVE

Do you have an enquiring mind? A thirst for knowledge and a desire to share and pass on what you have learned is a vital component of the freelancer's make-up. In fact, it is a huge privilege to be able to investigate and learn new things throughout your working life. As you move on to each new commission, so you must research and learn enough about the subject to pass on the knowledge to your readers. Even if you focus on writing about a particular specialism, you will always continue to increase your in-depth knowledge of the subject and you will look at new angles to present the information to new audiences. This job has its pitfalls but boredom is not one of them.

Try it now: Evaluate your listening skills

One of the most important attributes of the writer is the ability to be a good listener – and, most crucially, to listen without judgement. Try interviewing a subject and, apart from asking the odd question, allow them to relax and to ramble on as much as they like. Write up the interview and show it to them – they may be surprised at just how much information they shared.

NEWS NOSE

Can you spot the angle for a story in the everyday events and situations that surround you? Taking the mundane and the ordinary and being able to find something of interest within is an essential quality for a writer.

The outlook for freelance writers

There is a mixed bag of news for those thinking of making money from writing. Certainly, if you go on statistics alone, you might very well give up on your ambition right now. According to the last big survey of more than 25,000 writers carried out by the UK's Authors' Licensing and Collecting Service (ALCS) in 2005, typical earnings from writing alone were less than £5,000 per year; that's less than a quarter of the typical wage of UK employees at that time.

Of course, there are those who do make a good living from writing but there is real inequality within the profession, with the top 10 per cent of authors earning more than 60 per cent of total income, while the bottom 50 per cent earn less than 10 per cent of total income.

The reality is that most writers end up supplementing their income from other sources such as a second or part-time job, or household earnings from a partner. In fact, only 20.3 per cent of UK writers earn all of their income from writing.

The overriding message from the survey seems to be: don't give up the day job just yet, especially as the first ten years of a writer's life are the hardest, particularly for the 24 to 34-year-old age range. If you survive the early years and become established, with better connections and greater experience, your potential earnings increase substantially until your mid-fifties, when they start to decrease again.

And if you're hoping that, post the 2008–2010 recession, the rates of pay have soared, I'm afraid you will be disappointed. Freelance fees appear to have plateaued at pre-recession rates, if not fallen. To make matters worse, editors and publishers are taking advantage of the countless hopefuls trying to break into the industry to pay minimum amounts or even to use writers as interns, namely for experience only and without payment.

Yet it is not all doom and gloom. The growth of the Internet, 24-hour radio and television broadcasting together with the emergence of new media has opened a new age of opportunities for writers, or 'information providers', as we're now known in the techie world. There seem to be countless possibilities and new openings if you are receptive to this new medium.

Better still, the emergence of blogs, e-zines and online content does not appear to be damaging the traditional market unduly. Despite the understandable caution of publishers in this precarious economic climate, more books than ever are being published and new magazines are being launched all the time.

All this is music to the ears of the freelance writer, because, although we all want to produce the best-quality writing we can at all times, in order to earn adequately, it is quantity that takes primacy for the freelancer; you need a wide variety of outlets to which you can sell your ideas if you are to make a living.

So the outlook is not as bleak as it at first appears. There will always be a demand for writers who can communicate ideas and who write to a professional standard, but those who will do best in the freelance market are those who either have a second source of income, at least initially, or those who are prepared to go looking for multiple outlets to which to sell their ideas.

Remember this: Package your ideas effectively

You may be the best writer and you may have the greatest ideas, but unless you can sum up those ideas in a succinct and persuasive package, the public will never know. No matter what the project is, fact, fiction, television show or travel guide, you should be able to sum up the concept in a couple of sentences.

What to write

So now you have thought about *why* you would like to be a professional writer, but have you considered *what* it is that you want to write? For many, elementary as it may seem, this is the biggest question – you wouldn't believe the number of times in writing workshops I've been told, 'I know I can write, but I just don't know what yet.' If you find yourself in that situation, by the end of this chapter you should have a clearer idea of where your strengths and ambitions lie.

As we have already established, the market for freelance writers is actually pretty buoyant – this is a good time to consider making money from writing. First and foremost, you need to identify which branch of the media you would like to focus on, and then look at other genres which might be a second string to your bow. It's never wise to put all your eggs in one basket, so multiple outlets are the order of the day for the successful freelance.

PRINT MEDIA

Whether you want to write books, or for magazines or for national and/or regional newspapers, there are in fact transferable skills that can be adapted for any of these markets. Clearly, you need to break into one of these media first before you can start writing across the other genres. However, to take one example, writing a book and then selling articles to newspapers and magazines on the topic (thereby at the same time publicizing your book) is a sensible way to get as much income as possible from one idea and the research involved in the initial project.

The ALCS survey compared writing income (professional authors – i.e. those earning more money from writing than any other source – let's say commercially successful writers then) across different genres of the print media. Its findings showed that writing for television was the most lucrative career, with median (typical) earnings of £39,419 per annum, and this figure soared to £73,000 per annum if you write for the popular TV soaps. Theatre and film writing typically earned its authors £20,000 per year while writing fiction books, for newspapers/magazines or for audio/Internet earned writers typically around £13,000 (children's non-fiction is slightly higher at £15,531 per annum). The lowest earners in the print media are authors of non-fiction books, with a median writing income of £8,000 per annum.

Try it now: Find out what's out there
Take a stroll into your local newsagent's or bookstore or surf the Web to get some idea of just how many outlets for the written word there are. The breadth of topics covered and the styles – from high-brow to gossip rags – is just astonishing.

WRITING FOR BUSINESS
This is quite a specialized field in that you have to be able to translate what corporate executives are saying or doing, sometimes in quite technical fields, so that their clients or the general public can understand. A specialism is not essential but it helps if you can get to the nub of the situation and structure stories from material that the client might see as random or un-newsworthy.

Writing for business tends to be better rewarded than other forms of writing because you are dealing with corporate clients who are used to paying higher rates. They are also used to paying for first-class travel and good expenses, so the fringe benefits can also be better.

GHOST-WRITING

This is for the more experienced writers, but it is worth considering if you can work well with occasionally difficult or busy people, are able to interpret and express others' views, and will settle for being out of the limelight. Ghost-writers are often paid higher advances for books than they might claim as a solo named author because publishers are willing to pay extra for the celebrity name or person in the public domain. Obviously, you would be receiving only a percentage of royalties, but depending on the 'author' and the subject, it can still be a rewarding exercise.

Try it now: Determine your direction

Spend some time thinking about your writing style, your subject matter and your areas of expertise/interest, and try to decide which media best suits those attributes, and which genre you are most drawn to.

WRITING FOR NEW MEDIA

This is a relatively new and untapped market offering plentiful opportunities for writers. There is everything from blogs and website copy to e-zines and ebooks to consider. Official figures on what you might earn are hard to come by, and I would not put too much store by the adverts suggesting Internet writers and marketeers can earn six-figure salaries. Nonetheless, it's another string to the writer's bow, and social media is definitely a tool that writers need to use to market and publicize their other writing.

Key idea: New media versus traditional outlets?

New media via the Internet is a vast and untapped market for freelance writers and the good news is that, despite early fears to the contrary, it does not appear to be unduly damaging more traditional publishing outlets such as books, magazines and newspapers.

Whether you feel you have a novel in you or you'd like to share your knowledge in a non-fiction book; whether you are passionate about writing for children or want to brush shoulders with captains of industry; whether you want to combine a passion for travel with a writing career or you need your voice to be heard through the medium of broadcasting – all of these outlets are valid ways to earn money for the determined writer. There is bound to be a genre that will suit you and your writing ambitions.

Case study: Jonathan Telfer, Editor of *Writing Magazine* and *Writers' News*

'I think most of us feel like we were born writers and for the most part that's where we get the drive to keep at it in the face of rejection. Among *Writing Magazine* readers it seems to be that passion, rather than anything else, that motivates them to write, which isn't to say that nobody expects any payment for it.

'Professional writers need perseverance, a thick skin, obviously exceptional grammar and, probably more so these days, some PR and marketing skills, because every pitch you make to an editor is effectively a sales pitch. The divide between what you might call commercial and creative writing is narrower than it ever used to be.

'Even those who write out of passion and a pure love of writing want to get published. The search for validation drives a lot of us, as in, "someone somewhere thinks my work is good enough to print." There are people who want nothing more than to write for themselves and never show it to anyone, but the majority, even of those who are doing it purely for the love of writing, are at some stage going to want to take it to an audience, to find readers for it or hopefully, even better, to sell it to a publisher or put it on Amazon themselves.

'It's a fabulous time to be a writer in some ways but, in others, it's more difficult than ever. The number of books being published keeps escalating, so it's more difficult to make your mark and it's more difficult to get accepted, but, on the other hand, doing it yourself has never been easier. For those writers who are planning to do it themselves, we've now got past a lot of the stigma of self-publishing, so the returns can be higher, and possibly better than they might be by getting published traditionally. So, it's a trying time for writers trying to keep on top of all these things but, if you want to make a go of it, the opportunities are definitely there.

'The problem is, of course, that it's easier for *anyone* to get a book out there, whether self-published, Amazon or ebook. The marketplace is growing so fast that it's more and more difficult to make yourself heard above the clamour.

'There is a big issue of quality control as well, particularly in ebooks. Interestingly, I think that writers are very concerned about this, but it doesn't seem that readers are as concerned. If they were, we would very quickly see a weeding out of badly written and badly researched books, and that doesn't seem to be the case. The chaff can do as well as the wheat, which isn't to say that anyone should aim for chaff. It's a concern for those who are putting their all into it and writing well: how to differentiate ourselves from those who are writing badly. It would be a shame if the reputation of e-publishing dragged down good e-writers, just by association. All we can do at the moment is to keep trying, keep standards high and keep doing it, and hopefully to rise to the top.

'Economically it's not a great time for journalism, but for journalists, again it's about finding new routes to market. A lot of magazines are restricting their freelance take and probably not increasing rates in line with inflation, which has been the case for many years. But there are still markets out there, and if you can't sell an article to a magazine, would it suit your blog and would it attract traffic to your blog that could then sell adverts on the back of it? Could you repackage themed articles into an ebook to sell direct to readers?

'Writers have to be more flexible than they were in the past. What we have to guard against is preserving the traditional just because it's the traditional. Try new approaches. Some will work, some of them won't, but better to have tried and failed than attempting to cling on to the same patterns of submission and rejection which we've seen for decades. And don't forget: publishers and editors are looking for people who understand the way things work now. Social networking, blogging and email marketing are now part of most writers' lives, so even if they make you feel uncomfortable at first, embrace them!

'I'm very lucky to get paid to write and edit. My entire life I have always loved words — shuffling them, juggling them and playing with them, so to be able to do that all day and every day hardly feels like work. It can be a lovely way to earn some extra money if it's not your day job and, if you are lucky enough to support yourself with writing eventually, even better.

For me, there have been some wonderful experiences – meeting authors I've had a long-standing respect for or sharing advice that I know has hit home with a lot of people; those things are always special but when you write for the love of it, it's all a joy. There are many reasons to attempt to get into writing or publishing but, if you don't have a love of words, I think you should probably find something better paid.'

Remember this: What's stopping you?

For every good reason you may have for wanting to earn money from writing, there is always a reason holding you back. Can't find enough time? Don't know where to start? Don't have any contacts? These obstacles will be addressed in the following chapters. So what's really stopping you?

Key idea: Don't give up your day job

In order to get freelance work, it is virtually essential to have some published work to show. While you are getting together that early portfolio, it is unwise to give up the salaried job, however tempting it may be, because you may not earn any money from writing for months or even years.

Focus points

The main points to remember from this chapter are:

* As well as being able to write, freelancers need certain personal attributes to be able to successfully work from home.
* Most writers rely on a second income to supplement earnings from writing.
* You need to source multiple outlets into which you can sell your work.
* New media and the Internet boom are producing new opportunities for freelance writers.
* Whatever your writing ambitions, there's a medium that will suit your skills.

Next step

Once you have decided which genre of writing best plays to your strengths and which others might make a good backup, you have to consider how you will generate the ideas to sustain your writing and how to identify the best avenues to market and sell your work; all of which will be discussed in Chapter 2.

2

Getting inspiration and selling your ideas

In this chapter you will learn:

- ▶ *Where and how to find inspiration for your ideas – from your life, from the people you know, from books and magazines, and from new media*
- ▶ *That, while your ideas don't necessarily have to be absolutely original, your angle – your individual approach – should be*
- ▶ *The importance of keeping abreast of your specialist subject area – knowing what the trends are and what your competitors are writing about*
- ▶ *How to pitch your ideas to editors.*

The only way that you can make money as a freelance writer is if you keep coming up with new ideas to sell. And, ideally, not at the end of a project – otherwise you have a fallow period between jobs – but several weeks before the end, so that you can pitch ideas and have a commission in place to start as soon as you've finished the last job.

To achieve this, you have to be generating new ideas much of the time. Although that sounds exhausting, it actually becomes second nature and you will find that you develop highly tuned antennae that pick up inspirations and storylines from numerous everyday sources.

That's important because there is no sense in waiting for that light-bulb moment when an original and outstanding idea comes to you – you could wait a very long time. You have to go after ideas.

In fact, it is not the quality of your writing that will get you commissions; it is good ideas that will secure you work (although you will obviously have to come up with the goods once you've been commissioned). A writer who regularly sends great ideas to editors will soon get their attention and be rewarded with regular commissions.

Key idea: Identifying a specialism

You do not have to be an expert in a subject to write about it. You simply have to have a real interest in the topic and know who to go to in order to ask the right questions. If you don't have a specialist subject, you can choose one.

Seeking inspiration

Fortunately, there are techniques that help you to generate ideas and to pursue the more worthwhile ones, and that help you to tap in to the rich source of material that is at your fingertips.

WRITE ABOUT WHAT YOU KNOW

This sounds like a cliché but it is nonetheless true; your first port of call when looking for inspiration is always to look at your own life. Naturally, it helps if you have some expertise or experience in a certain subject before you write about it, but that does not mean you have to be a leading expert in the field. It simply means you have to have relevant personal life experience in order, first, to convince a publisher/editor and, second, so that you sound authoritative, informative and interested to the reader.

Try it now: Look for inspiration

Once you start actively seeking feature/book ideas, the creative process snowballs and you will spot plenty of inspiring sources. This is why people who make their living out of coming up with ideas, such as writers and advertising executives, never seem short of new project suggestions. Put some energy into looking for inspiration and you may be surprised at how creative you become.

Ask yourself: 'Do I know what I'm talking about?' A brief word of warning at this point: your inner self-critic is initially likely to play down what you have to offer. Yet, you may be surprised at just how knowledgeable you are. If you work in a profession or specific field, or have wide experience of a certain sport or hobby, there is a good chance that you have a rich supply of material and a wealth of knowledge that could be of great interest to a more general readership. As a chiropractor, your experience of dealing with back pain could be of benefit to countless back-pain sufferers. One of the clients I helped while working as an editor for Writers' Workshop was a divorce lawyer, who wrote a book aimed at ordinary couples explaining the legal processes involved when a relationship breaks down (the book is selling very well). Your specialism may be hairdressing, bee-keeping or creating ornamental fishponds – all of these topics appeal to different audiences but there is a demand for informative articles/books on all of them. The fact that these subjects have been covered before is immaterial – people are always interested and editors always need to present the information as it develops in new and interesting ways.

The people in your life could provide a wealth of potential material – friends, family, colleagues all have potential. You will undoubtedly know people who have undergone exceptional experiences, whether it is surviving a disaster or serious illness, or an amazing feat of endurance or self-sacrifice. Perhaps an interview with them could form the basis of a feature to submit to a relevant publication. Perhaps a local paper would be interested to know that a hero of the Balkan wars of the 1990s is living in their midst. If there is enough depth to the story, could it even be the subject of a book?

Remember this: Research the market

Although it helps to write on subjects that interest you (if not, the copy tends to be flat and lifeless), you must still be sure that there are enough other people who share your passion in order to sell books. You must research the market.

Perhaps it is one of your family ancestors who has led a remarkable life and who interests you. The number of people researching their family history has boomed with the advent of research tools such as the Internet and television programmes such as the UK's *Who Do You Think You Are?* Life histories are a popular strand of the non-fiction market and a good story will sell.

And it doesn't just have to be people that you know. Perhaps a local organization has a story that is worth reporting – a local speech and language unit in the local primary school that's transforming young lives could interest an educational publication; or the amateur dramatic society that has prodigious young writing and acting talent might appeal to the entertainment pages of a local newspaper.

Try it now: Keeping a notebook

Most writers I know keep a notebook full of ideas. Whether you keep file cards or a notebook, keep it to hand for when you have a good idea – and jot it down while you remember. When out and about, some writers even take pocket notebooks or use mobile phones and voice recorders to make a note of a good idea – transcribing it into their 'official' ideas book when they get home.

READ VORACIOUSLY

You can get many ideas from reading newspapers and magazines. Many subjects that you see in print are covered regularly as they are always popular with readers; you simply have to come up with a new way of presenting the material – a new angle or hook to hang your idea upon.

Another approach is to look for real-life experiences that fit the profile of your chosen publication. Most newspapers and magazines like stories based around case studies, so if you have a strong human-interest story, you can base your article around that. There is an insatiable demand for new and interesting personal accounts, so keep your 'editorial' ears alert for good stories when talking to people.

Try it now: Get to know your rivals

Whatever your specialist subject, take a look at a few papers and magazines to see how other experts are using their knowledge to sell their writing. There will be columns by gardeners, chefs, astrologers and many more. How could you enliven those pages with your own expertise and style?

NEW MEDIA

Today's writer has to be comfortable using Twitter, Facebook, LinkedIn and other new media and online sites. It is the best way to keep abreast of what is happening and what is 'trending'.

If you are writing within a particular area of interest, then follow the big organizations and leading charities in that field on Twitter. Follow key individuals as well. Once you see what's trending for them, follow it up with broader searches on the Internet.

Similarly, make sure that you have a profile. Use network sites to promote yourself and your specialist interests. Make contacts with other journalists who are writing in your field or for publications that you want to write for. Subscribe to the media websites that advertise and promote jobs for freelance writers such as Gorkana – even if you don't apply for specific posts, it's a great way to see how the industry is changing and to keep abreast of what is wanted.

Getting a fresh angle

You do not have to reinvent the wheel. You may get frustrated when you see one of your ideas already in print, but actually it doesn't matter if a subject has been covered in a book or feature before – that simply shows there is an interest. What's important is *how* you present the topic. For example, John Gray's book *Men are from Mars, Women are from Venus* enjoyed sales of more than 40 million copies. It was not that books about the differences between the genders had not been written before (in fact, they were plentiful), but the angle that men and women are so different they might as well come from different planets was completely original. It was a concept that people could grasp straight away.

Often, what you are doing is taking a straight (and sometimes dull) news story and giving it a feature angle that will make a lot of people want to read it.

Remember this: Ideas can come at any time!

I always keep a notepad beside my bed so that I can jot down any ideas that come to me in the night as dreams. In that early-morning half-awake, half-asleep state, you think you'll remember, but dreams are elusive and you may well forget the detail if you don't commit it to paper immediately.

Knowing what is topical can also help you to come up with a fresh angle. If there is an ongoing outcry in the press about politicians and their expenses, perhaps this could be the hook for your feature on teaching ethics and values in education for the *Times Educational Supplement*. Talk about discovery of the God Particle by CERN scientists at the Large Hadron Collider could be an opening for a feature in an esoteric magazine about non-duality and monotheism. Using something that is currently uppermost in the public's and in editors' minds as a hook for your story and your topic is a good way to get your ideas noticed.

Although having a specialist area that you write about can help to generate ideas, you must always keep a weather eye on what other outlets there are and where you can go next if you exhaust your existing expertise. As a freelance writer when my children were young, I wrote features for mother and baby magazines and books on raising sons and juggling family life – all topics which were of great interest to me at the time. Now my family is grown, I have left that market and moved into other areas of interest, currently spiritual living and health. While new ideas come to you at different stages of your life, and as you develop different specialisms and areas of interest, you will probably also need to actively search out what the market is demanding and supply that, too, if you are to generate enough work as a freelance writer.

Try it now: Brainstorm Ideas

Writers have always used tried-and-tested techniques to help generate countless ideas. One of the best is to brainstorm by jotting down ideas in a stream without judging or editing. Simply write down whatever comes into your head and what follows from that – follow the flow of thought. The sifting process comes later but rest assured, many writers have discovered great feature or book concepts from a brainstormed idea that may at first have looked outlandish.

Pitching ideas

We have established that editors are looking for great ideas, but what is the best format to get these feature suggestions and book proposals noticed?

Let's take it as read that the idea you are pitching is either picking up on a trend that has not been covered before by your target publication, or it is a popular topic but presented in a really refreshing way. The other given, of course, is that the idea fits the publication that it's aimed at and you have researched its needs fully.

The pitch itself is your one shot at getting work, so make it good. Naturally, to give yourself the best chance of success, you should send it to the commissioning editor for that section of the magazine/newspaper and use their name, pointing out the specific page/section that you have in mind for your idea.

You can use many different formats for pitching to editors. Nearly all use a head-sell (where you use a striking headline followed by a brief stand-first – that little snippet of running commentary that comes before your introduction). Some writers use bullet points to keep their idea succinct; others use a narrative style where the writer discusses how they hit upon the idea and why it's right for this publication.

There is certainly no one right way to pitch, although you will soon discover the preferred style for individual editors once you start working for them regularly. The current trend with national newspapers and bigger magazines is for a head-sell followed by a précis of the idea including details of any experts/case studies you might plan to include, but styles go in and out of fashion, so it is trial and error to start with.

If you are new to an editor, then it helps to mention your credentials in terms of writing experience, but it's not normally necessary to send cuttings unless they are requested.

Key idea: Targeting a specialized audience

Narrowing the subject area of a book may sound counter-intuitive but targeting a specialized audience actually increases sales. Perversely, by knowing your audience and tailoring the information closely to their (and your) interests, it means more readers will identify with its content and buy it.

If you have access to good, high-resolution (minimum 300 dpi for print) photographs to accompany the feature, this can be very persuasive, as it saves the editorial team not only the headache of picture research, but a lot of time. The format to send images in is JPEG, TIFF or GIFF.

Once you've sent your email pitch, you can follow up with a brief phone call to see if the editor is interested. There's every chance that they will not have read your pitch, as it will be lumped in with the countless PR bumph, random queries and spam, but a follow-up call outlining a strong feature will get their attention – but check that it is not approaching press day or your call will not be welcome.

When pitching, the golden rule is to never send more than three ideas. This is the optimum number for features as it shows you are more than a one-trick pony but you will not look desperate. And don't be surprised if the editor goes for the idea that you believe is the weakest – you don't know what other factors are affecting their decision.

Remember this: You are responsible for your career

It's good to have people within the industry who are on your side, but if an agent, publisher or editor promises to help 'build your career', take it with a pinch of salt. These professionals are representing many writers and their interests, and you are just one among a number that they will be promoting. In-house staff also move on regularly, so pinning all your hopes on one editor in a specific position is dangerous. The bottom line is that you, and you alone, are responsible for building your career.

Hard though it may be to let an idea go, if the editor says 'no' to an idea, unless you have a good relationship with them, then you have to accept that, on this occasion, it was not right for that publication. Try to sell it elsewhere, repackaged for the new publication, but if it still does not sell, it may be that the idea was not quite as good as you at first believed.

Case study: Liz Bestic, freelance health writer for national newspapers

'I've been a freelance on and off for 25 years. You have to keep up with the flow to come up with fresh ideas. You have to watch to see which way the tide is turning. You need to be aware of where your next market is because it's moving so fast.

'When I was starting out, there was a rush of expansion in local authorities and charities. I saw the opportunity and started writing and doing communications for local authorities and charities. Later, I noticed there were loads of outlets for women's health writing so I moved away from the charity sector into health.

'Finding angles is important. If you're going to send a story into the *Daily Mail* [UK newspaper], you have to think about what they are actually covering at the moment. You have got to read their "Good Health" section from top to bottom. Scour the pages and try to understand what they're looking for. At the moment, for example, I know that they're looking for cancer good news stories and stories on the "big five" health issues – Stroke, Cancer, Blood Pressure, Heart Disease and Diabetes.

'When you're pitching ideas, go to the person who is actually buying them. Nowadays, they actually like you to write a little synopsis of the story when you pitch. You have to summarize the story in a short précis and explain that you've got a case study who will say *this*, and you're interviewing *these* experts. You must sum up the idea in a precise way.

'If you're going to pitch to someone like the *Mail*, they want complete professionalism. You need to be absolutely on top of your game. So you need to go online and check your story has not already been used by someone else. There is no excuse for pitching them something that's already appeared. If they've covered it in the news section, that's OK because you're taking a news item and turning it into a feature. If they're interested, the sort of questions they'll ask you is: "Has this been covered by anyone else before?" You need to know that, so, before you pitch, you have to Google the condition and the treatment and make sure it's not been covered by a competitor.

'I get a lot of ideas from PR companies, so get yourself listed on their distribution lists. Twitter is the place you ought to be. You should be following all the top newspapers on Twitter to see what's trending. You need to be following independent people, too – because I'm interested in politics, for example, I follow a lot of political commentators – but whoever is in your area, see what they're saying and what's trending for them. If something is trending, I look it up to see what's going on. You have to be open to everything that's out there.

'Angles change along with fashions and trends. It is about looking, observing and seeing what's happening and being up-to-date with all the new technology because that is the future. Everything is going on Kindle. If you're young and you're new to the game, you need to be familiar with Twitter and Facebook etc. because otherwise you're not in the loop. If you know how to use Twitter, then tweet – "I'm writing a feature on such and such."

'I look online a lot and read a lot of articles online. If you're pitching to magazines, you need to read the magazine and understand who it is aimed at. Ask yourself: "Would I want to read this story?" If you are passionate about it, you will sell it better.

'If you like writing for print, you have to notice what's happening with newspapers. Recently, I noticed that *The Times* and *The Sunday Times* had started using this advertorial-based, newsy 16-page pull-out called *Raconteur*. I emailed them and they invited me in and now I do quite regular work for them that has involved interviewing Richard Branson and Lord Steel. It's been great.

'You should go on LinkedIn and update your profile every week. I'm also on a lot of media database sites like Gorkana – one of the big national newspapers was advertising for someone to write for Kindle recently, so there's that kind of work around, but you need to be in the system. It would be on a freelance contract basis which is nice because then you can do other stuff as well.'

'If you're doing regional stuff, which is great fun but poorly paid, you need to be on the lookout for interesting people. There is no shortage of people to write about. Just talk to people and chat to them – everybody has a story. Regional papers want interesting or eccentric locals. People are happy to talk to you because everyone loves getting their picture in the paper.'

Focus points

The main points to remember from this chapter are:

* ✻ A successful writer needs to keep coming up with good ideas.
* ✻ Editors buy ideas, not writing.
* ✻ Look at friends, family and colleagues as a source of case studies and feature ideas.
* ✻ The Internet and social media are essential tools for keeping abreast of what's 'trending'.
* ✻ You must be completely familiar with your target publications and pitch specific ideas tailored to them and their readership.

Next step

Once you have come up with a good feature idea or concept for a book, you then have to start the research to ensure that there is both a market and an outlet for your idea. In the next chapter we explore how to tailor your feature/book suggestions to the right audience and the right publications or publishers.

3

Finding material

In this chapter you will learn:

- ▶ *About the wealth of resources available to you as you research your ideas*
- ▶ *How to use the Internet wisely*
- ▶ *About the ways in which interviews – and the supporting quotes they provide – can enrich your work as well as making it more marketable*
- ▶ *How to conduct an interview efficiently and appropriately.*

Once you have established that you have a viable idea for a book or feature, and you have some target editors lined up, the next step is to do some research to find out whether there is enough material available to support the feature or book idea. After a trawl of the Internet and newspaper archives, you have to ask yourself if there is anything new to say on the subject or do you have a new angle of approach? If the answer is 'yes' to either of these questions, you can start to research in earnest.

You need to gather information from various sources to inform and flesh out your feature or book idea. This can be a lengthy process, and for a professional journalist for whom time is money, identifying what is salient and what's not, and knowing when you have enough, is a skill that you will have to develop. It's a temptation to keep looking and finding out more and more, but you can only use so much in an article, and it is better to find what's most useful as quickly as possible and then stop, than to keep adding to a pile which then has to be sifted and edited anyway.

Luckily, with today's communication networks, there has never been an easier time to research your project. There are countless resources to call upon and it is worth exploring as many as possible. Alternatively, you can cherry-pick the resource that best suits your particular writing project. For example, if you were writing a personal history of your great-grandfather who fought in the First World War, you would focus on genealogical resources, the local history section of your local library, military and regimental archives and interviews with family members. Looking at national newspapers and the Internet in general would probably be a waste of your time, unless your great-grandfather was decorated, famous or infamous.

Try it now: Keep a record of your sources

You must have a system in place to keep your research sources to hand in case an editor or publisher needs to know provenance of your facts. Try setting up folders in your email accounts and online in the Favourites or Bookmark sections, and keep all your research sources in these for each project.

The following are some of the resources that you can call upon in your quest for background material.

The Internet

The World Wide Web has made a writers' job so much easier with its almost inexhaustibly supply of research material on every topic imaginable. It also offers the most immediate information available. However, you must exercise some caution when using the Internet as a research tool. Firstly, you must make sure that your source is reliable. Many websites offer at best opinion or speculation rather than fact, and are at worst erroneous. If you find something that you think is useful, always cross-reference it against other sources.

Remember this: Check the date

Always check the date that research information was posted on a website. There is no point thinking you have cutting-edge information if the startling revelations were posted on the site five years ago.

The most reliable sources of specialist information are the professional organizations, governing bodies and leading charities in the field. There is plenty of interesting information on their sites, but you will also find details of their press office – contact them directly for more targeted information or for experts to interview.

The Web also provides useful resources and alert sites for writers. Not only do these sites provide access to experts and professionals such as university lecturers and other specialists, they also mean you can get help from fellow journalists and public relations people. Some are general resources while others focus on specific areas ranging from technology and travel to health and food.

Books, magazines and newspapers

Despite the popularity of the Internet, books and magazines are still a valuable resource for writers that should not be overlooked. If you are writing on a specialist subject in particular, there is a good chance there will be a book or article on that precise subject that you can read.

If buying research books for an article takes up so much of the fee that it ceases to make economic good sense, then don't forget that you can use specialist and public lending libraries. You can also get copies of relevant magazine features from the back issues department of specialist titles. For example, if you are writing for a niche market, such as vintage Italian motorbikes, then contacting the editors of the newsletters/ magazines for the Ducati, Laverda and Benelli owners' clubs could prove a useful source of first-hand knowledge.

Local newspaper archives are often stored in their offices or at the local lending library. The librarian should be happy to help you to get to grips with the microfiche system. Similarly, national newspapers have online archives that you can search for free in some instances, though others charge for the service. However, it can be a worthwhile investment if you are regularly researching feature/book ideas, which, as a busy freelance, should be the case.

Key idea: Avoiding plagiarism

Getting additional research information from written material such as books and magazines is fine if it helps you to further understand the subject, and you can even take the odd quote from a book/

feature, as long as you provide a reference. However, if you use the text rather than interpreting it for your readers, then that is plagiarism and it is illegal.

In order to reprint copyrighted material in your book, you need to seek permissions, and the sooner you start the better because it can sometimes be a lengthy process. If you're quoting from a book or article, contact the publisher; to reprint lyrics from songs, contact the record company. Most companies are happy for you to reprint as long as you give a full credit. Occasionally a fee is involved.

Interviews

Introducing the voice of an expert or the narrative of a real-life case story into an article or book can lift your writing and add interest or gravitas in equal measure. So do not be afraid to interview people in the course of your research, as it can be a powerful addition to the facts and statistics that you unearth.

In the case of celebrities, public figures and leading authorities in their field, they will usually be the subject of the whole article and you will submit it as a profile or interview. Far more often, however, you are interviewing people who have information that you need in order to understand the subject better or to illuminate a point you are making within a feature, and you will use only a few quotes.

If you want unique and up-to-the-minute material, it is best to interview experts within the field. You can contact the press office of professional associations, governing bodies, educational institutions and charities who can put you in touch with a relevant expert. Some press officers may be reluctant to help you unless you already have a firm commission, however.

You can also contact experts directly by contacting research universities or enthusiast clubs and asking if one of the professors, lecturers or experts is willing to be interviewed.

Try it now: Look for other viewpoints

If you are interviewing a number of different experts for a feature/book, then try putting what one has said to the others to see if they agree or not. This can either lend strength to an argument or sometimes it produces a controversy that you can weave into your copy.

INTERVIEW OPTIONS

By far the best way to conduct an interview is face-to-face using a recording device (I take shorthand notes for backup, but this is a dying skill). You can glean a great deal more from an interview when you meet in person. It provides you with background colour for the feature – what they were wearing, their attitude, their home – more importantly, it gives you a better chance to get inside their head. You can also read their reaction to questions more accurately than by telephone.

If this option is not available to you, or if you only want to ask a few questions or simply need help understanding a complex concept, then you do not need to invest the extra time demanded (or the money) by physically going to interview someone face-to-face. In this case, it is perfectly adequate to interview someone over the phone or, increasingly, by Skype.

Interviewees rarely have the time to speak to you when you first ring, but they are usually happy to talk if you make an appointment to ring back at a more convenient time. You might like to forewarn them about the content of the interview so they can give some forethought to their answers.

An alternative is to do an interview via email. The advantage of this is that the subject has a chance to give serious thought to their answers and will be able to include everything that they want to cover. The disadvantage is the quotes can sound somewhat 'pat' and they can lack the conviction of 'off-the-cuff' comments. This, of course, is not a problem if you are interviewing someone for background technical information.

Emailing is, nonetheless, a very useful way of getting the main points and major queries covered and it is also useful if your interviewee is short of time or travelling, as they can get around to answering the questions at any hour of the day or night that suits them.

Try it now: Interview a friend

Good interview technique can only be achieved by practice. The more people you interview, the better feel you will have for putting the interviewee at ease, when to ask the most penetrating questions and how to wind it up successfully. If you are new to interviewing, practise on a friend or colleague. Keep the interview to a maximum of 10 minutes (that's about 1,000 words' worth of quotes) and then write a profile in about 750 words, quoting the subject.

INTERVIEW TECHNIQUES

Whether you are going to conduct an interview in person or by telephone or Skype, here are a few tips on good practice:

▶ Forewarn your interviewee about how much of their time you are likely to take up in advance of the interview.

▶ On the day, make sure you have contact details for the interviewee in case there is an unforeseen change in your plans and you have to call them en route to the interview.

▶ Arrive promptly, and dressed appropriately for the occasion and location.

▶ Have all your equipment ready (with spare batteries for your voice recorder) and make sure you are familiar with how to use it before the interview.

▶ Check that your voice recorder is picking up their voice adequately and there is not too much background sound before you get stuck into the interview.

▶ Initially, talk a little about how you see the interview unfolding and engage in some small talk, about your journey for example, so as to put the interviewee at ease before you launch into the questioning.

- Be pre-prepared with open questions (those that require more than a simple 'yes' or 'no' answer) but be relaxed about diverging from your plan if the interviewee leads you off onto a different but relevant (or juicy) subject.

- Don't be afraid to show your ignorance. If they say something you don't understand or mention a name you don't know, it's perfectly acceptable to ask them to expand on that.

- You can ask blunt questions – they usually elicit straight, and often interesting, answers.

- If someone tells you something 'off the record' (and explicitly tells you it is such), then you should honour this. More often than not, they get so carried away with the conversation that everything they say is on the record and can be used.

- You are trying to get the best from your interviewee, so coax them into revealing as much of themselves and their subject as possible.

- Always leave the difficult questions to the last and get yourself off the hook by explaining that it's not you who's asking, but the readers who want to know... yes, *that* hoary old chestnut.

- If interviewing ordinary people for case studies, be gentle. They are not trained in interview techniques and sometimes the subject matter can be delicate or upsetting.

- Always check how the interviewee would like to be credited – that is, their name and title. In the case of personal stories for case studies, check if they want to use a pseudonym to protect their identity or whether you can use their real name.

Remember this: Respect your interviewee's time

Whether you are interviewing celebrities, experts or professionals, it's worth bearing in mind that these are extremely busy people and it is only fair that you prepare your questions in advance and that you keep the number of questions to an essential minimum. Once the conversation is in full swing, and if they seem happy to continue, then you can deviate into other areas.

WINDING UP AN INTERVIEW

Always remember to thank your interviewee for their time at the end of the interview and ask if you can get back to them if there is anything that you do not understand when you transcribe your recording or that needs greater clarification.

At this point, many interviewees ask if they can see the copy before it's published, usually under the guise of wanting 'to check the facts'. Occasionally, this is mutually beneficial – for example, when you want to check you have got it right or if you want to build a future relationship with the subject. However, in the vast majority of cases, especially as a freelance writer, you are not in a position to promise copy approval. Once you have delivered your copy, subeditors may alter it or cut it as they see fit, and you have little or no control over that.

You can agree to allow them to check it for accuracy but explain that this may not be the final version, although direct quotes will not be changed (but may be cut). Alternatively, if you just want to play for time and hope they forget, you can always suggest that you are unsure of editorial policy on this matter, and that you will check with the editor.

Taking it further

Interviews not only help with research and furnish you with quotes, they can also lead to more business. If you are specializing in a specific field, you can build good relations with your interviewees by sending them copies of the published article/book and thanking again for their help. This keeps communications open – sometimes these people then become the source of more information and ideas for future features.

Keep their contact details – you never know when you may need an interviewee again in the future. If you follow key interviewees in the press or on Twitter, for example, you may find that they have done a U-turn on a certain subject and that in itself might make the basis of a new feature idea – why the new stance?

If you're in a specialized field, your interviewees may be influential and, through the relationship you have built with them, corporate writing jobs could follow. So, wherever possible, keep the relationship with an interviewee on a positive note and keep it open, so that you can always go back to them in the future.

Key idea: Making good ideas work for you

The only way to make money as a freelance is to make each good idea work hard for you. So once you have a good story idea, you need to research different angles so that you can sell the same story to several different outlets, say a local newspaper, a specialist magazine, a business-to-business title and a tabloid, each with a different spin.

Case study: Ian McCann, Editor of *Record Collector* magazine and former Chief Subeditor of the *News of the World* magazine

'To establish whether or not an idea has legs, do your homework. Boring, obvious advice, but having been on both sides of the writing/ commissioning divide, it amazes me how many writers offer material that your magazine wouldn't want in a thousand years.

'You have to understand the publication you're aiming at. Try to find out what commissioning editors are looking for – not just before you approach them with a piece but before you've done a lot of legwork in putting the story together. If you know other writers who work for them, pick their brains; it's not cheating, it's networking.

'Failing that, a pleasant email or call to the editor in person might elicit the information you need, after you have read a few issues of the mag. But bear in mind just how busy they may be: if you are contacting someone on the national press, do it early or mid-morning; later on, they'll be too snowed-under chasing that night's deadline to even read your email.

'Time really is money, so it's a good idea to take a few moments to calculate just how much work it is likely to be. If it's going to take you a month of chasing to track everyone down and you're going to end up earning £28.79 for it, forget it unless you feel passionate about the subject. Yet again, you never know where a feature might lead; I did a small piece on the pop band East 17 that paid about £60 and I ended up getting a few thousand pounds' worth of work out of it.

'If a celebrity is your main subject matter, then chances are you'll be able to obtain most of the quotes direct and build the feature around them. But a celeb is only going to talk to you if they have something they want to promote; which means they're not only speaking to you, but everyone else. So ask yourself how you can make your piece stand out.

'Research is often fairly easy to do thanks to the miracle that is Google. Plus a celebrity's PR *should* take pains to send you a press release, biography and even recent cuttings. Writing about music or movies, it's often a doddle to uncover an interviewee's history and you can gen up on them in seconds. But it's also worth checking cuttings about other celebs that worked with the interviewee: a different perspective might reveal a question you should ask that might catch them off guard and draw a response that is more interesting than the usual pat answer.

'Sometimes you are told never to broach a particular subject – he won't talk about his sexuality, so don't ask – and then when you get into the interview, you might find that the subject is actually more than willing to talk about that verboten issue.

'To persuade a celeb to tell you anything meaningful, discover their personal interest. For example, I interviewed Jermaine Jackson. He'd been corralled into supporting some Motown Hits package and was going through the motions. However, get him on his favourite hobby – motor racing – and he'll talk ten to the dozen. After that, he relaxed and was a far better interviewee. Tom Jones, on the other hand, can be fresh and engaging, despite so many years of being asked about having knickers thrown at him. The secret is to question him about music – he is so used to talking about being the last man standing, his sex life and Las Vegas, that when he talks about music, about which he retains enormous enthusiasm, he comes alive and then he'll start revealing more of the real Tom. Basically, it's a matter of knowing which buttons to push.

'Make sure you know how long you have got and ask the easy questions first if the interviewee is sensitive. That way you have some usable material before you drop the bombshell towards the end that upsets the applecart. Most interviewees realize you are only doing your job, although some may take offence.

'To keep the story fresh and interesting, consider whether your piece is newsworthy. Is there some reason for doing it – an anniversary, an event, something you know that nobody else has bothered to find out? Is there someone else you can speak to connected to the main subject who might provide a different perspective? Could you dream up sidebars that are tailored to the subject matter of the magazine you are working for? Does the interviewee have a health charity that they want to draw attention to, which you can feature in a sub-piece about celebs who have suffered from a similar affliction? Are there unseen photographs which would help sell the story? The more possibilities you uncover, the greater the likelihood of your piece getting the green light.

'There is no doubt that a lot of commissioning editors want to see some new revelation about a celebrity or band, but it's also true that many don't. The fact is that a new interview with Paul McCartney, no matter how bland, will always be more saleable than a think piece that proves conclusively that The Beatles were rubbish. If you are intending to destroy the accepted wisdom about your subject, make sure you can back your argument up and only approach publications that are willing to buck trends.'

Focus points

The main points to remember from this chapter are:

* The reliability of your research sources is imperative.
* Invest enough time in research but know when to stop.
* Don't rely solely on the Internet – use other resources, too.
* Quotes from experts and high-profile interviewees lends gravitas to features.
* Good contacts from research can supply future ideas and sometimes leads to further work.

Next step

Now we have the preparatory work of coming up with ideas and the supporting research done, let's take a look at the various outlets available into which you can sell your writing, starting with print media, such as magazines and newspapers.

4

Writing for magazines and newspapers

In this chapter you will learn:

- ▸ *How to pitch an idea to the editor of a print publication*
- ▸ *About the various kinds of feature found in newspapers and magazines*
- ▸ *How to get the most financially out of a single story by reworking it for different outlets.*

Assessment: Evaluate your suitability as a writer for newspapers and magazines

Answer the following questionnaire to get some idea whether or not you are suited to writing for magazines and newspapers:

1 Are you able to come up with lots of ideas for features and interviews?

   YES   NO   PROBABLY (with practice)

2 Do you like researching background information to include in your features?

   YES   NO   PROBABLY (with practice)

3 Are you comfortable interviewing and empathizing with people, even if you may have to ask difficult questions or cold-call?

   YES   NO   PROBABLY (with practice)

4 Can you write to a prescribed length (word count)?

   YES   NO   PROBABLY (with practice)

5 Can you adjust your style for different types of publications?

   YES   NO   PROBABLY (with practice)

6 Are you able to make time in your schedule if you have to meet a tight deadline?

   YES   NO   PROBABLY (with practice)

7 Can you write well under pressure, for example, to length and to a deadline?

   YES   NO   PROBABLY (with practice)

8 Can you come up with an interesting angle as a 'selling' hook for your feature idea?

   YES   NO   PROBABLY (with practice)

9 Do you have the confidence to pitch your ideas to an editor?

   YES   NO   PROBABLY (with practice)

10 Are you able to bounce back from rejection and go on to approach other publications with your ideas?

   YES   NO   PROBABLY (with practice)

Scoring: Give yourself 2 points for each question to which you answered 'Yes'. Give yourself 1 point if you answered 'Probably (with practice)' and 0 points for all 'No' answers.

Assessment: If your score is:

15–20 points: You are ideally suited to journalism and should have no problems finding ideas, writing under pressure, and getting your features accepted for publication.

8–14 points: There are certain aspects of writing for magazines and newspapers that you are going to have to master if you want to break into freelance journalism. However, with practice this goal should be achievable.

0–7 points: Your love of writing may be better suited to another genre of publishing that is less pressurized. Nonetheless, if you are determined, the practical advice in this chapter may help you to realize your ambitions.

Of all the fields of professional writing, in many ways magazines and newspapers represent the greatest opportunities for novice writers to get published and paid simply because of the sheer breadth of topics that these titles cover. There are specialist, hobbyist magazines and consumer glossies, trade journals and consumer titles, not to mention local, regional and national newspapers.

Realistically, writing for national newspapers and the glossy newsstand magazines is usually the pinnacle of a journalist's ambition and it is an extremely competitive market to break into. Nonetheless, if you set your sights a little lower, there are plenty of magazines and local papers that rely on a mixture of contributions from professional writers and unsolicited material. These publications are ideal for cutting your teeth on and gaining experience and they pay, albeit the rates are often quite low.

If you have specialist knowledge to share or good feature ideas and you can supply a well-written, informative or entertaining article that is superior in style to the usual reader offerings, then you stand a good chance of acceptance by these specialist magazines.

Remember this: Consult industry guides and handbooks

To find out contact details and further information about the magazines and newspapers you plan to approach, there are two main guides that writers use – *The Writers' & Artists' Yearbook* and *The Writer's Handbook*, both of which are published annually and are available from bookshops. These are useful to writers as they provide helpful information about hundreds of magazines and newspapers, but do make sure you have a current edition. For contact details for trade magazines, in-house and flight publications, try *Benn's UK Media Directory*, *Willings Press Guide* and the *Guardian Media Guide*, all of which can be found in local libraries.

Making a pitch

Selling an idea to a magazine or newspaper editor is known as 'a pitch'. If you decide to approach your local and/or regional newspapers, you could think about reporting on local events, interviewing local celebrities, craftspeople or artists, writing reviews of restaurants or plays, or covering local sports events. Perhaps you have a local history story that might be of interest.

Remember this: Get the name right!

Invest time in getting the correct name and title of the relevant editor before you pitch an idea. It's worth calling the switchboard to check these details before sending your feature pitch since open-addressed emails, or those sent to predecessors, are not taken seriously.

Normally, features for newspapers are time-sensitive, so you must pitch ideas in advance to the appropriate editor – larger-circulation newspapers may have different editors for specific areas such as sport, features, arts and politics. Monthly magazines have longer lead-in times, so feature ideas must be pitched well in advance of any season or event that the feature relates to.

Send a succinct email outlining your idea, as editors are extremely busy people. If they express interest, you can always go into greater detail in a phone call or follow-up email.

Here are a few tips on how to pitch successfully:

▶ Address your pitch to the relevant person, using their name and title.

▶ Come up with a catchy title that amuses and stimulates interest, while hopefully encapsulating the essence of the feature.

▶ When outlining your feature idea, it is useful to provide a little background information about the general situation, plus the specific focus your feature might take.

▶ Cite any specialists you might interview or case studies you might include.

▶ As an unknown quantity, it is important to establish your credentials for writing the feature. So, if you have specialist knowledge, qualifications or unique access to information/an interviewee, then make this clear. You must also show that you can write, so if you have writing experience, you can also mention this.

▶ Suggest a reason why your feature should be published. This is known in the trade as a 'peg' or 'hook' to hang your idea on. So, for example, 2012 is the Diamond Jubilee of Queen Elizabeth. This is the perfect hook for countless feature submissions ranging from those with a nostalgic base to an article about the merits of a long service in one field compared to the current trend for a 'portfolio' career.

▶ Proofread your covering email and any material you might submit. You only have one chance to make a good impression on an editor, and spelling or grammatical mistakes in your submission will count against you. By the same token, make sure the layout is clear and that presentation is good.

Remember this: Don't bombard the editor with ideas

Enthusiastic though you may be, do not be tempted to bombard an editor with ideas. Put one to three good ideas into an initial approach email. Wait until you have received feedback or a response before sending any more ideas. If an editor feels that they are being badgered, they will start to ignore your correspondence, even though it may contain some good ideas.

Irrespective of whether you are writing for a trade magazine, a consumer title or a free newspaper, you need a hook on which to hang your feature idea. By this, I mean that you offer the editor a reason for accepting the feature. So, it may be something timely – for example, a feature about romance can be best justified in an issue that is on sale around 14 February, Valentine's Day. Similarly, you can use other annual events such as Christmas, Thanksgiving, New Year, Halloween, Easter, Harvest Festival, Guy Fawkes Night or the changing seasons to stimulate a feature idea and to strengthen its appeal to an editor.

Once you have been commissioned, then is the time to discuss details such as word count, deadline and rate of pay. Do not be self-conscious about asking for this information in writing – it is simply professional.

If an editor is reluctant to commission you (they sometimes prefer journalists with a proven track record or they have used before), you could always submit a couple of examples of the sort of reviews or features you have in mind, together with a covering email. An interview with someone of particular interest to the readership often wins good results as this saves getting a staff journalist to set up an interview and write it up – and it might be someone they have not considered or have been unable to get.

Try it now: Familiarize yourself with the 'standard' features

Most magazines and newspapers carry some regular features (these are often flagged up on the contents page under that very heading) and this type of feature is required in every issue. So familiarize yourself with the regulars in suitable magazines and then come up with ideas of topics that could fit neatly into this category. It's a good habit to get into.

Writing a feature

Whether you have been given a commission or have decided to write your feature and submit it speculatively ('on spec'), there are two major issues that you will need to address:

1 *How long should your article be?* If you have not been given a word count, then think about the page space allocation you are hoping to fill. Magazine features tend to cover one to three pages. You should therefore be thinking about writing in the region of 750 words for a one-page feature, 1,500 words for two pages and 2,250 words for a three-page feature. In reality, anything much more than this is unlikely to be accepted as an unsolicited approach; and if you send an article that's over 4,000 words, you are jeopardizing your chances of acceptance as it would have to be subbed down to the right length and this requires time and effort by in-house staff.

2 *Have you considered what genre of feature is most likely to be accepted by a magazine or newspaper?* Obviously, if you are writing for a specialist title, then the subject will be self-evident. Even so, within this field, there are different types of styles that you could consider.

'HOW TO' OR SELF-HELP

Always popular, not only with the specialist or hobbyist magazines but also with women's weeklies and local newspapers, a practical, skills-based article is perhaps one of the easiest ideas to sell. If you have specialist knowledge, that is better still, and you should make it clear that you are an expert with knowledge to share when you approach an editor. An expert who can write is a rare commodity and always in demand in publishing.

Usually a 'how to' article takes the form of a brief, general introduction to the subject followed by more practical information. If it is a skill-based feature, such as how to bake the perfect muffin for a cookery magazine, then step-by-step instructions may be required within the text.

UPLIFTING

Upbeat tales of 'triumph over adversity' are always popular with newspaper and magazine editors. Find a triumphant story about a local person for the local newspaper or a pertinent success story for a specialist magazine (e.g. horse-rider survives accident and overcomes obstacles to ride again for an equestrian title) and you stand a good chance of selling it.

The public has an unquenchable thirst for real-life stories and you may even have your own personal tale to tell. Anything to do with health, parenting, education or personal development is popular at the moment.

FILLERS

These may not be what you dreamed of writing, but there are people who make a regular income, albeit small, from sending small written items to magazines and newspapers. These might be: letters, humorous anecdotes, handy hints, or gaffes (such as the funny things people say). Although you may not get a fortune, pro rata, these fillers are paid quite handsomely, so if you have a gift for writing witty quips, and you can send them out in quantity, it could be a reasonable earner. More importantly, it might just be the springboard into broader journalism that you have been looking for.

COLUMNS

You may be tempted to write and submit an opinion piece or an observational column since they are such fun to write. However, in reality, these regular slots are almost exclusively given to experienced journalists or to someone in the public eye such as a celebrity. If you enjoy this style of writing, explore it in a blog format and, who knows, you may be spotted (see Chapter 9).

Remember this: Get the most out of your story

If you are to get the maximum return on the time you have invested in researching an idea and interviewing people, then you need to sell the story more than once. If you have sold it to a monthly glossy, there is nothing to stop you rewriting it from a different angle and selling the story again to a local newspaper or a smaller specialist magazine.

Stretching fees

Freelance feature writers do not get paid a fortune. The way that most jobbing journalists make money is by making a feature idea work hard for them; that is, by selling the same story, rewritten with a different emphasis, to several different outlets. Many explore the overseas markets as well as their own domestic publications. In this way, the effort put in to researching an article is rewarded more fully. This is not the same as selling the same feature to several different publications, which is most certainly frowned upon unless you've made it abundantly clear that this is the case.

Remember this: Hit your deadlines

If you are writing for magazines and newspapers, you have to be able to hit deadlines. It's no good being able to produce a masterpiece if only you had more time. An editor will often want a feature turned around quickly, so if you are going to pitch an idea, be ready to start immediately so that you can meet your deadline. Do not wait for the go-ahead and then have to set up interviews and start your research.

Many freelance writers augment their income by working shifts across the print media, whether it's as an in-house writer or subediting (checking copy and making it fit house style and the page). This may not be what you set out to do, but subediting shifts not only provide a backup income, but are often a useful source of contacts with commissioning editors.

Rates and conditions vary widely across magazines and national and regional newspapers. The National Union of Journalists (NUJ) publishes a guide to freelance fees (available online) which can be very useful when negotiating rates for feature writing and day shifts, but be warned – I know lots of freelancers who are accepting fees way below the NUJ recommended minimum, and sadly a publisher/editor has no shortage of choice if you stick to your guns.

Key idea: Getting paid

Smaller magazines and papers are notorious for paying contributors late. In fact, freelance writers can wait several months from delivering copy to getting paid, and many end up spending an inordinate amount of time chasing payments.

Although it is a creative career, you must stay on top of your accounts. And be prepared to deal directly with the accounts department, so that you do not sour your relationship with the commissioning editor. Most freelance writers are a member of a professional union such as the NUJ so that you have a little more clout when it comes to chasing payments should things go seriously awry.

Finally, make sure you register with the Authors' Licensing and Collecting Society (ALCS). In this way, you will receive payments from secondary uses of your writing such as photocopying, and a share of uncollected fees for non-registered writers. You must of course keep the Society's list updated with your published works, and you will receive an annual payment. It's not a fortune but not to be sniffed at either.

Key idea: Contract publishers

Contract publishers – who produce magazines and similar for non-publishing organizations – may pay considerably more for work used in a given category of magazine than direct publishers would. Sometimes it pays to look further afield.

Case study: Jean Elgie, Editor of *Your Week* and Associate Editor of *Weight Watchers Magazine*

What makes a successful feature pitch?

'I always prefer submission enquiries to be made by email as it's so hard to keep on top of all forms of contact. Although I receive on average 120 emails a day, if someone does call with a pitch idea, I always say: put it in an email. No one really uses the post any more, apart from publishers with a view to possible book extracts.

'Although I would consider a submission if it were not addressed to me personally, I would wonder why the journalist hadn't bothered to find out whom to pitch the idea to.

'Within a submission for a proposed feature idea, I would expect a journalist to include a headline/cover line as that helps to attract my attention. Then I would want to see a 150-word maximum outline, covering the approach and who the experts are that he/she would interview plus any interesting statistics that would support the submission. For example, if it's a health feature on stress, I'd want to see how many people are affected by stress in the UK.

'It is also very helpful if a rundown of experts to be interviewed are cited in the submission. For example, when it's *Weight Watchers Magazine*, we have to steer clear of nutritional therapists and go for registered dieticians or nutritionists. This is because all facts/statements have to be backed up by robust sources.

'With regard to information about the journalist themselves, if I don't know them, I'd like information on whom else they write for and whether they are a member of the Guild of Health Writers, in the case of a health feature. Ideally, I like to see cuttings accompanying a submission if the writer is unknown to me, though these wouldn't necessarily represent what their copy is like on receipt. I've had copy in from some writers I've not used before that has needed considerable rewriting.

'That said, I'm always keen to try someone new as I strongly believe in using different voices. It can also help with new ideas as, although one tends to use familiar writers, new ones can shake up the mix.

'The lead in times on a monthly magazine are ridiculously long. We need feature ideas at least 12 weeks ahead of publication date. I have sometimes held on to a good idea, though, to use in a subsequent issue.

'For me, the most compelling aspect of a successful submission is a good handle above all else. For example, we have to cover weight in the health section of every issue, so it helps to have a new approach or angle. And with beauty or travel, I'd be looking for clever ways to cover what is a fairly standard staple in any women's magazine.'

Focus points

The main points to remember from this chapter are:

* ✳ Identifying the right outlet for your writing is crucial and will maximize your chances of acceptance.
* ✳ Be constantly vigilant for sources of feature ideas whether it is from the world around you, reading magazines and newspapers, or preempting seasonal or forthcoming events/anniversaries.
* ✳ Practise writing features to a variety of different word counts and to various deadlines.
* ✳ Interviewing people is a skill that you will have to master if you want to write for magazines and newspapers.
* ✳ It is essential that you prepare well before you pitch an idea to a magazine or newspaper editor – you only have one shot at it, so be ready.

Next step

Perhaps the immediacy and short deadlines required by writing for newspapers and magazines is not for you. If you prefer longer lead-in times and a more in-depth approach, you should read the next chapter which looks at writing non-fiction books.

5

Writing non-fiction books

In this chapter you will learn:

▶ *How to write an effective synopsis for a non-fiction title*

▶ *About the system of advance payments widely used in non-fiction publishing*

▶ *The importance of tailoring your style to your target audience*

▶ *About the frequently used features found in self-help and 'how to' books, such as case studies, lists and focus boxes.*

Assessment: Evaluate your suitability as a writer of non-fiction books

Answer the following questionnaire to find out whether or not you could be the author of a non-fiction book:

1 Do you have an area of specialization or expertise?

       YES NO PERHAPS

2 Do you have a personal story to tell?

       YES NO PERHAPS

3 Can you organize your thoughts, ideas and research?

       YES NO PERHAPS

4 Are you thorough and tenacious when researching a subject?

       YES NO PERHAPS

5 Can you write to length and to a deadline?

       YES NO PERHAPS

6 Are you good at making complex subjects accessible to others?

       YES NO PERHAPS

7 Are you able to find a new take on a well-reported subject?

       YES NO PERHAPS

8 Do you have a desire to help others by sharing your knowledge?

       YES NO PERHAPS

9 Can you write informatively without sounding didactic, dry or hectoring?

       YES NO PERHAPS

10 Do you have a network of contacts within your area of expertise?

       YES NO PERHAPS

Scoring: Give yourself 2 points for each question to which you answered 'Yes'. Give yourself 1 point if you answered 'Perhaps' and 0 points for all 'No' answers.

Non-fiction has always been seen as something of the poor relation to its more attractive cousin, fiction writing. Yet, for those wanting to make money from writing, non-fiction may prove a more promising arena. Despite the gloom of the economy, there are exciting opportunities in this field and none more so than the growth area of self-help and 'how to' books.

The audience for this budding market are readers wanting to:

▶ Increase their specialist knowledge

▶ Bolster personal, social or professional skills

▶ Resolve personal issues.

So, if you have an area of expertise or specialist interest, and you are able to come up with a new and innovative approach to an existing, popular topic, you may well be able to interest a publisher. After all, interest in the subject has already been proven by the plethora of books/magazines already available on the topic. So you do not have to reinvent the wheel or persuade a publisher of the marketability of your idea; you simply have to offer them a new hook to hang the idea upon.

Key idea: A buoyant market

This is a relatively buoyant market with certain niche markets, namely cookery and gardening titles, even topping the bestseller list. All of us need 'expert' advice at some time, so you could put your specialist knowledge to good use, whether it's about steam trains or making organic chocolate cakes.

Unfortunately, the downside to specialist knowledge is that experts are very often adept in their area but that does not make them good writers or give them a natural ability to effectively share their knowledge. The greatest gift of the self-help writer is the ability to take complex or specialist ideas and to make them accessible to the general public or hobbyist enthusiast.

If you can write well and have an interest in a topic (you do not even have to be an expert on the subject – as long as you have access to and can interpret the information of specialists), and can convey this information simply and effectively to the reader (actually this is essentially the job of a journalist), then you could be ideally placed to write non-fiction in this genre.

Try it now: Make a subject accessible

Can you explain a complex specialist idea to someone with no previous knowledge of the subject? Why not take a single concept or principle and write a definition in about 150 words and try it out on a newcomer to the subject. Having read your words, get them to explain the concept back to you to make sure that they have not only grasped the idea but have understood it fully.

A good synopsis

Although non-fiction books hold good potential for writers, it is still a competitive market, so you have to optimize your chances of getting published. Essential here is providing the commissioning editor with a good synopsis.

Here are the key aspects that a synopsis should contain:

▶ Give a clear idea of how you will convey your specialist knowledge in the book – what form will it take?

▶ Tell the publisher what sets it apart from its competitors and what makes it unique.

▶ Make sure they know that you have a clear idea of your target audience – for example, those new to the subject or more experienced readers.

> Finally, you need to set out your credentials – why are you the best person to write this book and what are your strengths as the author?

Keep in the back of your mind the fact that publishers want to get good value from their authors – if your book does well, they may want a series of titles from you on the subject. Keep some ideas up your sleeve for future publisher meetings.

If you ring all the right bells, you could well earn yourself an advance because non-fiction editors know the markets and can estimate the audience a book might appeal to and its marketability. They also know that, with good in-house editors, a book can be shaped into what they want – a luxury that is not really available to fiction publishers – which means they are more inclined to back a good idea even if the author is an unknown quantity.

Effectively, however, a publisher is investing in you when they pay an advance since you keep that money whether or not they sell a single copy (you only have to repay it if you fail to deliver the book). In order for the publisher to recoup their outlay, they must do their utmost to maximize sales through good design, marketing, publicity and so forth, but it is still a gamble. So somewhere in your synopsis or covering letter you have to be able to convince them that not only will the book sell well, but that you are able to deliver what you promise.

Try it now: Write a synopsis

Work up the synopsis for your book and send it to agents and publishers. If you are rejected, gauge response and, if it's consistent, revise your ideas accordingly. If you get a commission, get writing.

Getting an advance

Unlike fiction, if you produce a good synopsis that can convince a publisher of the merits of your book, you might get an advance so that you have some income while you write. According to *The Writers' and Artists' Yearbook Guide to Getting Published*, and in my own experience, a typical advance for a specialist non-fiction book is in the region of £0–£5,000, usually paid in three instalments (namely, a third on signature, a third on delivery and acceptance, and a third on publication). But before you can secure that advance, you must persuade potential publishers to take a chance on you.

Deadlines allowed on commissioned non-fiction books are usually in the region of three to four months. When calculating whether or not the advance will cover you to write full-time for that period, remember that you only receive a third at the start and the second tranche on delivery, so do not use the full advance figure in your calculations.

Key idea: 'Earning out'

If you have been paid an advance on your book, you will not earn any royalties until the advance has been recouped – what's known in the trade as having 'earned out'. If you secure a large advance, you may never 'earn out' through sales, but hopefully you have been paid enough to make the exercise worthwhile, and, once on the shelves, you just never know – it may take off!

High-yielding ideas

As with all types of professional writing, the best way to earn money is to make each idea pay for itself several times over. So, if you have written a non-fiction book and been paid for it, you should then approach specialist, hobbyist and/or women's consumer magazines. With a book under your belt, you are now viewed as an authority on the subject and you can sell articles (specifically tailored to the audience for each magazine) to features editors, who are obliged to fill pages on this topic each week or month and who are always looking for new ideas and angles.

Another possible spin-off from specialist non-fiction is the biography. As an authority on a certain subject, you may well know the leading lights of that specialism. Access to a prominent figure and having their trust is a persuasive pitch for a commissioning editor and, if you can convince them that you have unique access to information that will give the book a commercial edge, then you could well get yourself another commission as a biography writer.

Format

We have established that one of the crucial elements of a persuasive synopsis is knowing how best to convey your knowledge to your reader – what form your book will take. The purpose of self-help and 'how to' books is:

- To give readers new abilities
- To help them along a developmental route
- To show them ways to overcome perceived or existing problems
- To acquire specific skills.

This means that the advice and knowledge you impart has to be practical and easily understood. Unless you are talking to an experienced readership, you must make complex and unfamiliar concepts and language accessible and comprehensible to novices and those who are less knowledgeable.

When giving thought to how you might compile your specialist knowledge into a book, bear in mind that self-help books tend to fall into two main categories, namely step-by-step books and modular books:

- ▶ **Step-by-step books** often take the reader through a programme so that they progressively learn new skills. It has a progressive style which is particularly effective for 'how to' books but can also be used for books on DIY, self-improvement, fitness, sports, diet and health.

- ▶ **Modular books** can be broken down into clear component parts, which together give the reader a new skill or solve a problem. Each component roughly takes a chapter.

Content

The tone for non-fiction, self-help books is normally informal, reassuring and sympathetic while remaining authoritative. Keep the language simple, with full explanations of any technical or specialist terms you might use.

Key idea: Keeping your audience in mind

It is crucial that you know your reader. If you have a person in mind, you can tailor your style, language and tone exactly to that audience. If the readership is similar to yourself, then imagine you are coaching and supporting a friend. Clearly, a book aimed at young pregnant women is going to use a different style and tone to one aimed at retired gardeners.

Self-help and 'how to' books use a variety of different tools to keep the pace spritely and to keep the reader involved, and primarily to stop the book becoming a dry textbook. The following devices are some that you might like to consider using in your book. Their inclusion shows a potential publisher that you have thought about ways to engross your reader and to engage with them, which in turn helps to persuade the publisher that this might be a viable project.

You can include:

- ▶ **Case studies**   Readers love anecdotal stories and are reassured that they are not alone if they read of others in a similar situation. Clearly, a positive outcome is the most beneficial as it has the effect of uplifting the reader.

- ▶ **Statistics and facts**   Bold or startling facts can capture the reader's attention and introduce drama into a subject that may not at first sight appear that exciting. They are also useful for supporting a point that you are making.

- ▶ **Exercises and quizzes**   Reader participation is what sets self-help and 'how to' books apart from other kinds of non-fiction writing. Participation strengthens a reader's confidence in their ability, so interactive pages are very popular.

- ▶ **Checklists and lists**   These are useful when you want a reader to remember a series of important ideas, to make sure they have taken note of every element of a process or system, or to come to a decision about something.

All of the above participation techniques are effective in this style of book, but you must ensure that you explain clearly to the reader what is being asked of them and what they are likely to get out of it. If the participation involves giving answers, you must also help them to be able to evaluate their results.

Remember this: Technical writing is better paid

If your book involves technical writing, you should get a higher rate flat fee than for a normal non-fiction self-help book.

If you get the formula right – with the correct balance between expert advice, inclusive tone and reader participation, and you tailor your book to a niche audience, then you are making it easier for a publisher to see how the end product might be marketable.

Try it now: Write a set of instructions

Often 'how to' books include step-by-step instructions that must be clear and easy to understand if your reader is to be able to follow them successfully. They must also work. Why not write out a set of instructions for a practical exercise as it might appear in your book and get someone to follow them to the letter – do they understand them, can they follow them properly and do they work?

Case study: Liz Dean, Consultant Commissioner for illustrated non-fiction books at Octopus Publishing Ltd

'I look for a really strong idea in a synopsis but it needs to have validation as well – so clearly define your concept and explain why you, the author, are the best person to write about this particular subject – is it because it's your trade; because it's a personal longing (something you've grown up with that you really want to express and explore, for example); or because your book has a historical hook that you feel is of value but which has been neglected? Publishers can see whether an idea has got potential if they understand an author's burning passion for what he or she wants to write.

'If your synopsis is going to stand out, you have to be able to express the book idea in a couple of sentences, to be succinct, because, more often than not, the commissioning editor or publisher has to go and discuss that idea with just a couple of colleagues, or even a whole boardroom of people depending on the size of the company. And that group may include sales directors, marketing people and so on who may not necessarily have an editorial background, but who need to get the idea in a nutshell.

'If the author can't explain the concept of the book in a couple of sentences, you can't expect the commissioning editor or publisher to then sell it to everyone else within the company, who then have to go out to bookshops and sell it, and so on. Understanding this chain of communication is helpful.

'For young authors (I talk to people in their late teens and early twenties like Ross Bartlett), I think you almost expect them to have a platform through Facebook or Twitter because the younger generation have grown up with that technology. But with older writers, they are usually very clear about the contact that they want to have with the rest of the world and it may just be through workshops or organizing talks and meetings. Publishers want evidence of an author's desire to express themselves in the world even if it's on a one-to-one basis or in more intimate settings, but not to just expect the publisher's marketing department to go and make them famous. It needs to be a co-creation of the writer with their publicist and editor in communicating their work and getting it out there.

'I wouldn't be put off someone if they didn't have 500 Facebook friends, for example. After all, it's hard to quantify just how much these media sell books. But being willing to seek endorsement for your writing will help, and that doesn't mean spending all day on Twitter.

'Writers can do much to help themselves such as researching a bit more about what a publisher does. Sometimes it's obvious you're getting multiple submissions and an author is just sending them out to everybody. Clearly, they've bought a copy of the *Writers' and Artists' Yearbook* and they've gone through it like a dose of salts. You need more mindfulness about what each publisher does, and show your awareness by including a covering letter or saying in your email, "I've noticed you publish these particular books. My book is kind of like your title *XX*, but it's unique because of these elements in my writing... and because of who I am." This gives the publisher a point of reference because the commissioning editor may be thinking, "Where does this fit in my list?" Not just, "This is a great book."

'Publishers are a lot more specialized than people outside the industry realize. There's a huge catalogue of books on offer from the big publishers, but they might have six to ten commissioning editors responsible for little chunks of that. So each commissioning editor is actually quite specialized in their field. If you're going to write to somebody, that's really good to know. Even if it's an exploratory email saying, "This is the subject I'm writing a book on. Is this something that you're usually interested in? Is this something you usually publish?" I think that would help to narrow down the submissions, so just submit to say three publishers that you've done some real research on. It's just a lot of wasted effort otherwise. If you're a good writer and you've researched your book, you should be able to research a publisher. That shows your skill and publishers really appreciate people who are dedicated.

'And, lastly, commissioning editors want to know what's new. If you have a particular interest and you sense a trend – it could be a new kind of crochet or a different type of meditation you have discovered – stuff that you're excited about, it's worth putting forward. Bring something new to the table. Find a twist – something that makes it different. Publishers appreciate that.'

Focus points

The main points to remember from this chapter are:

- Expert books are a good market with a ready and apparently insatiable audience.
- Publishers are more likely to pay an advance for non-fiction books in this genre.
- A good synopsis might secure you a deal so that you have an income while you write.
- Once you have written a self-help book, you are considered an authority on the subject and there are other spin-off writing projects that could earn additional revenue.
- Knowing which elements to include in the format and style of your book can make it a more marketable proposition for a prospective publisher.

Next step

If you feel happier writing the longer manuscripts of non-fiction books rather than short features but you would like to give your creative side some exercise, perhaps the next chapter on writing fiction will be of interest to you.

6

Writing a novel

In this chapter you will learn:

▶ *About the challenges faced by fiction writers*

▶ *How to optimize your chances of finding a publisher for your novel*

▶ *How gearing your novel towards a particular genre – crime, romance and so on – can boost your chances of getting published*

▶ *The importance of creating a memorable and likable central character.*

Assessment: Evaluate your suitability as a fiction writer

Answer the following questionnaire to get some idea whether your creative bent qualifies you for writing a novel:

1 Do you have a fertile imagination?

      YES   NO

2 Do you like researching background information?

      YES   NO

3 Are you an acute observer of people?

      YES   NO

4 Do you have characters in mind to populate your book?

      YES   NO

5 Do you have specialist knowledge that can help to inform your novel and make it credible?

      YES   NO

6 Can you be a ruthless judge of your own work?

      YES   NO

7 Do you have a story to tell?

      YES   NO

8 Can you be disciplined and set aside enough time to write a complete novel?

      YES   NO

9 Can you create believable characters and settings?

      YES   NO

10 Do you have any way to market/publicize your novel that might appeal to a potential publisher?

      YES   NO

Scoring: Give yourself 2 points for each question to which you answered 'Yes'. Give yourself 0 points for all 'No' answers.

Assessment: If your score is:

15–20 points: Well, they say everyone has a book in them – perhaps it's true in your case.

Fiction is the glamorous side of writing and there are countless would-be novelists among us. In fact, you could be forgiven for thinking that novel writing is a lucrative line of business given the success of blockbusters such as Stephenie Meyer's Twilight series or J.K. Rowling's Harry Potter series, or even given the sheer number of novels on the shelves of bookstores.

However, the reality is that making serious money from fiction writing is almost impossible. There is simply so much material on the market that publishers do not feel the need to pay advances for fiction (except for certain named writers). That effectively means that you have to produce the whole manuscript, which could easily take you six months and probably more, and then submit it on spec before you stand a chance of getting a financial offer.

For that reason alone, as an unpublished novelist, it is unrealistic to hope to make a living solely from fiction writing. Of course, you might write fiction as a bolt-on to a salaried job or as another aspect of a writing career (there are plenty of journalists-turned-novelists such as India Knight and Zoë Heller to name but a few). Who knows, your manuscript might just be the one that strikes a chord with a publisher and stimulates a big advance and a major marketing campaign, although the odds are definitely stacked against this, irrespective of how beautifully you write.

The wonderful thing about fiction, though, is that, despite these discouraging facts, many people still choose to write and get huge fulfilment from it, even if the financial reward is elusive. So what can you do to improve your chances of getting published and getting some remuneration, albeit non-commensurate, for your efforts?

Why write a novel?

This seems like a very obvious question but you'd be surprised by how few authors analyse their motives for writing before they start the project. Yet, it is important to identify what is motivating you so that you can establish the role it plays in your life.

If on closer examination you realize that really you want to write a novel purely for self-gratification, as emotional therapy, to get it out of your system or to leave a legacy, you should recognize that, while these are all valid reasons which should not prevent you from writing your novel, they do not necessarily make it a good financially proposition.

Equally, I would caution against writing a novel simply as a means to earning a lot of money because, for the vast majority of writers, this is not going to happen. However, there is some middle ground where you can marry your enthusiasm and passion for fiction writing with a few techniques to maximize your chances of the end product producing a cash reward.

Try it now: Start writing!

If you are going to write fiction, then of course you must plan it, but actually getting that first chapter down on paper is the most important step. Don't let your inner critic prevent you from letting the words flow (you can always refine them later). So stop procrastinating and get started. Time is money.

Optimizing your chances of publication

First and foremost, you have to recognize what a potential publisher is looking for. The majority of works of fiction are between 70,000 and 200,000 words, so if your manuscript is very wide of this mark, be it too long or too short, you are compromising your chances of acceptance. You should aim for somewhere in the region of 120,000 words.

Remember this: Does your story make a novel?

Given that a regular literary novel is around the 120,000 words mark, are you sure your idea for your novel is substantial enough to support this sort of length?

If a publisher likes what you have written, their first reaction is to think about how and where the title will sit, not only in their catalogue but on the bookshelves. Can your title be classified by one of the accepted categories? Would you describe it as a thriller or crime novel? Could it sit on the shelves with other romantic fiction? What about sci-fi or horror, sex or popular, humorous or historical fiction?

Key idea: Getting your novel noticed

Be clear about your aims for your novel and why your voice is the best one to tell the story. There are around a million manuscripts sitting in the offices of publishers in London and New York at any one time and you must be sure that your manuscript merits reading and acceptance.

A few years back, publishers could not get enough of what was fondly called 'chick-lit', and if you submitted a good manuscript in this genre at that time, you would have substantially increased your chances of acceptance and payment. If you were to try to sell 'chick-lit' now, you would be well behind the power curve. Genres of fiction go in and out of fashion, and being able to identify what is selling and write in that vein makes good business sense. Of course, no one wants to think of their work of art in such vulgar commercial terms, but, frankly, trends in reading habits are a fact of life, and if the theme of your novel can be tailored to coincide with the popularity of a particular genre, so much the better.

The marketing angle of your book is of the utmost importance to a publisher, so once they have identified the genre, a publisher needs to know that it will appeal to a wide audience. To this end, you must make sure that you have a clear idea of who your reader is and thus make sure that your book is something that your target readership will enjoy. Identifying what elements of your book will please your readers is another aspect of its marketing that you should be able to convey to a prospective publisher.

Key idea: Make your novel fit a genre

Can you fit your idea for a novel into an accepted and popular genre? It makes it more marketable if so, and that will increase your chances of selling the manuscript to a prospective publisher.

Writing coaches always tell novice authors to write about what they know. It has been heard so many times that it is starting to sound trite. Nonetheless, the truth is that, if you write about something that you have personal experience of or a passion for, that knowledge gives your book an authenticity and added appeal. If the subject is something that interests you, then there is a good chance that there will be other members of the public who share your interest, so you have a ready-made audience. The jockey-turned-writer Dick Francis had a long and successful career writing novels set in the racing world. Perhaps you are a recreational pilot and your novel could be based in the exciting arena of aviation. If your hobby is cake decorating and you are wondering how that might appeal to a wide audience, don't be down-hearted. Who would ever have predicted the enormous popularity of 'Aga sagas', which are essentially stories of family life in the British middle classes? It's hardly rock 'n' roll but it sells.

Readers love to learn something new when reading a novel, so your specialist knowledge of something, whatever it may be, could give that added extra that might just swing the balance in favour of acceptance from a publisher.

Try it now: Write a blurb

If an author is unknown, readers buy books based on the cover (over which you have little or no control) and the cover blurb. Take a look at the blurbs on the back of some of your favourite books and now try to write the blurb for your own book. This précis is effectively all the marketing information that you would include in a synopsis for a publisher or agent.

More ways to skin a cat

Continuing the theme of sharing knowledge, you might want to consider writing creative non-fiction rather than pure fiction. This style mixes fact and fiction, and dramatizes true events and stories. It is a genre that is enjoying great success and far and away the biggest growth in creative non-fiction in recent years has been in the area of historical books, as witnessed by the runaway success of Hilary Mantel's *Wolf Hall*. It is a dramatized account of the life of Thomas Cromwell that vividly invokes life in Tudor England. Published in 2009, *Wolf Hall* sold 137,150 hardback copies in its first six months.

If you have a particular interest in a specific era (Bernard Cornwell's Sharpe series gave a vivid account of the Napoleonic Wars) or knowledge of a foreign land (Alexander McCall Smith's No. 1 Ladies Detective Agency series is set in Botswana) or a location closer to home (John Murray's novels are set in Cumbria), then you could weave a captivating story around your knowledge. After all, there is a growing market for creative non-fiction writers.

Fiction publishers are looking for books with longevity that will keep the public coming back to bookstores for follow-up stories, so your main character has to have the potential to move on to other tales if your first book does well. This may sound like putting the cart before the horse, but you are committing commercial hari-kari if you kill off your main character at the end of your first book. In fact, if you manage to hit the payload with a character that the public loves, a publisher will want to continue to furnish the readers with more and more books.

This supply-and-demand effect translates to popular non-fiction authors who extend their careers by moving into fiction when they have exhausted their real-life stories, for example the SAS adventure authors Andy McNab and Chris Ryan.

In truth, publishers usually use existing authors or professional writers to cover the add-on titles in a series. However, if you have an idea for a prequel or sequel to an existing favourite classic, then it could be worth approaching the publisher who holds the rights with a proposal and some sample chapters.

Tips for successful fiction writing

▶ As a new novelist, it is best to keep things simple for yourself until you gain experience. So it's probably easiest to stick to a narrative in the first person, a theme that you know and like, and a strong but credible central character.

▶ Characters don't have to be perfect – everyone loves a flawed hero – but don't make it harder for yourself by creating a central character that is hard to love.

▶ There are three classic plots that the vast majority of books fall into:

1 The **linear plot** where the action moves straight through the chapters, with the tension building throughout until it reaches a natural denouement at the end.

2 The **heroic epic** where the story follows the pattern of departure (leaving the familiar), initiation (crossing a threshold) and return (after sacrifice comes enlightenment).

3 The **mythic journey** which involves a character embarking on a quest that involves challenge and betrayal before the climax and resolution.

▶ Stick within these parameters, irrespective of where and when your story is set, and it will make your life easier.

▶ Give thought to the setting and time period. Will your plot hold water in these scenarios?

▶ Keep the action moving. A good novel is entertaining – it doesn't matter how good your characters, things have to happen to them.

▶ If you always keep the theme of your book in mind (prominently displayed next to your computer if you like), you can stay focused, and it will help to prevent you being led off at tangents and along dead-ends.

Key idea: A memorable character

If you ask people about their favourite books, it is the characters that they find memorable, not necessarily the story. So make your characters interesting.

Try it now: Revisit your favourite novels

Revisit some of your favourite novels and try to see what it is in each one (and whether there's a common theme) that makes them so memorable for you. This is the feeling you then want to evoke in your own book, irrespective of whether it is a completely different topic and style.

Case study: Philip Gooden, author

Philip Gooden is the author of the Nick Revill books, a series of historical mysteries set in Elizabethan and Jacobean London. He also writes 19th-century mysteries, including The Ely Testament. *He is a member of the Medieval Murderers group who together have written some eight titles for Simon & Schuster. He writes non-fiction books on language (and blogs on it at www.philipgooden.com) and his latest title is* Idiomantics.

Writing fiction as a career

'Some people do luck out but most people do not make a lot of money from writing fiction. Publishers are much more cautious than they were a few years ago. It won't stop people writing and that's a good thing in a way. It's encouraging that so many people still want to write.'

Improving the odds

'If you are looking at things in a narrowly commercial way, then genre writing is one of the least difficult ways in to fiction because it's generally accepted that various kinds of crime writing, to a lesser extent science fiction, and some types of romance fiction have very steady sales and occupy quite a large chunk of the market. If you are predisposed to one or more of those forms, I think that is a good way in. The market for what one might call general fiction, be it middle-brow or literary fiction, is harder to get into.

'I don't think you can take up genre writing without knowing a fair bit about it and without being a devotee yourself. I think you have to like the form and be well versed in it. To go into it in a rather cynical way and try to knock something off because it looks easy won't work actually.

'Crime is the biggest genre field. If you're going to write contemporary crime fiction, you need to have a fair amount of knowledge about how the police do things (you can find these things out – there are courses and books), but if you don't want to do that, you can go back into the past, where you don't have to be so precise about methods.'

Characters

'Series characters give you longevity. Certainly, it was the case with me when I started writing the series for Constable & Robinson. I think the publisher may have taken the first book as a one-off, but, after that, I had a two or three-book contract. That is really on the understanding that you'll take the same character and push him forward into the next adventure.

'Sometimes authors write themselves into a corner. Perhaps for chronological reasons or other reasons, they take the character as far as they can go, and then of course they have to go back and do some in-filling – they take an episode from the character's past, from an earlier era in that person's life or an earlier adventure. It's quite a good device but it can smack a bit of desperation.

'I think you've got to like your character and get along with him. You might find him amusing. To a certain extent, he's got to be a projection of yourself. That would apply whether a man writes in the female persona, or a woman writes in a male one; there will still be elements of yourself in him or her.

'I think you can enjoy creating the villain, too. There's an American crime writer called Lawrence Block that I like very much. He wrote a series of books about a hit man. To have as your central character a man who has a contract to kill people and to make him likeable, and not to make the reader shut the book or want justice for him in the end, is quite an achievement.

'In theory, you can actually make a series character who is really unsympathetic; it just depends how you approach it. The more you disadvantage the character in that way, though, the harder it is. I don't think you'd get away with making your main character a mass murderer without a single redeeming feature; it just wouldn't work.'

Professional tip

'I find a deadline and a contract is a great spur, or one does put things off. With a commercial publisher, the deadline is very important. There are not many writers in the J.K. Rowling position where the publisher is waiting on them.

'I think it's good to have a deadline. When I am writing something I try to get about 1,000 words a day done. I have a strip of paper with a running total on it. I put the date and the word total for that day down. If I've done 1,000 words each day, I feel I've done OK. One of the quite good things about that is that it's quite legitimate to say to yourself, I could be doing something else today or take a break of a day or two. Actually, if you have it on a sheet of paper in front of you, it's very visible. It goads you but it's beneficial in the other way in that, if you're writing pretty well every day, it's surprising how quickly it mounts up – the average-length book would be done in three months.

'The other quite useful thing I've found is to finish when you've got two or three more sentences left. You know when it's going quite nicely and you know what you want to put in the next paragraph or few sentences – if you break off at that point before you've completed what you have to say, it gives you a starting-off point for the next day.'

Focus points

The main points to remember from this chapter are:

✳ Fiction is rarely commissioned so you must have other ways of supporting yourself financially while you write your first novel.

✳ However well written your novel, the publisher is most interested in its marketability, so make sure it ticks the right boxes.

✳ Publishers want to get more than one book out of an author so the main character should be able to sustain at least three books.

✳ Creative non-fiction, which dramatizes real-life events, is a popular and highly marketable genre / route into fiction.

✳ Having a platform to market your novel can be a persuasive point in your novel's favour for prospective publishers.

Next step

As we have seen, most would-be novelists end up writing while earning money from other avenues. Let's look at other writing genres that might pay the bills while you get creative. Travel writing is the first port of call.

7

Travel writing

In this chapter you will learn:

- ▶ *How to choose a travel destination*
- ▶ *How to maximize earnings from each trip*
- ▶ *What makes good, evocative and saleable travel writing*
- ▶ *How taking photographs to accompany your travel writing will boost your earning potential.*

Assessment: Evaluate your suitability as a travel writer

Answer the following questionnaire to get some idea of whether or not you are suited to travel writing:

1 Do you have lots of free time?

      YES   NO

2 Can you write evocative copy which appeals to all five senses?

      YES   NO

3 Do you have the ability to talk to strangers and to communicate well?

      YES   NO

4 Can you assimilate into different cultures?

      YES   NO

5 Can you take good photographs?

      YES   NO

6 Are you comfortable travelling independently and being on your own?

      YES   NO

7 Are you comfortable eating unfamiliar foods?

      YES   NO

8 Have you got an adventurous streak?

      YES   NO

9 Do injections bother you?

      YES   NO

10 Do you have a specialism that has a wide interest/appeal?

      YES   NO

Scoring: Give yourself 2 points for each question to which you answered 'Yes' and 0 points for all 'No' answers.

Assessment: If your score is:

14–20 points: Travel writing would appear to be a good choice for you. Take on board the advice in this chapter and you could soon be earning from your travel adventures.

Travel writing is a fabulous way to earn a living or to supplement your income – you get to see the world and enjoy new experiences and cultures. However, it is undoubtedly a hard market to break into, largely because so many freelance journalists are trying to make a buck from their holidays or attempting to get their trips subsidized. Nonetheless, there are countless outlets for travel writing, as most specialist as well as consumer titles carry travel features, so there is always a demand for good and unusual travel stories.

So, if you have the freedom to be away from home frequently and perhaps for extended periods of time, then travel writing is a great way to find interesting stories and to get paid – but, most importantly, to have fun doing so.

Realistically, you are not likely to get commissioned unless you have some published travel writing to show to a prospective editor. It may well be the case that you will have to see your first trips as a loss leader, just so that you have some material to work up into features to submit. But where should you start?

Try it now: Read travel books, watch travel programmes

Read travel books and features and watch travel shows on television. Then think about which features you enjoyed and which did not work for you. In this way, you can identify the style(s) that you would most like to emulate.

Choosing a destination

If you choose a well-trodden destination, then you can be pretty sure that it has been written about on countless occasions, so you are making your objective of selling a story all the more difficult. Why not choose somewhere that is off the beaten track or that is a bit more unusual.

Think of your specialist interests/knowledge and pick a destination that might tie in with that. For example, if you have an interest in spiritual living, then why not visit the centres of traditional Ayurvedic healing in Kerala, and submit your story to one of the mind, body and spirit titles? Whatever your specialty, there will be a few destinations that are perfect for you.

While you are getting your foot in the door, you are likely to be paying for your travel yourself, and hopefully recouping this at a later date when you sell your stories. So, you need to choose somewhere that is financially viable for you. If you shop around and are prepared to travel at odd times, there are affordable options available for most destinations.

Key idea: Travel writing is not just about tourism

Travel writing does not simply have to involve writing about a location. You can write about local characters, specialities of the region and so on, and sell those ideas as features, too.

Try it now: Read up before you go

Background research on a destination is never wasted, so read as much as possible before going on a trip. Anything written on the place, from novels to travelogues, can help to give you some insight and a better idea of possible angles for your features.

Before you go

Don't wait until you are *in situ* before starting your research. Broad background reading before you go – travelogues, geography and history books, even novels – will help you to make informed decisions about what to investigate and, in the long run, will save you valuable time once you are there.

If you are looking to pitch ideas to a specific publication on your return, make sure you are familiar with its style and audience so you can look for angles that might appeal while you are travelling.

If you have identified people that you would like to interview, for instance, then email them before leaving home to set up a meeting. Most people are helpful and keen to be interviewed, especially by someone who has travelled a long way to do so. If you leave it until you arrive to sort out the interview, you risk them being unavailable and you wasting valuable travelling time on logistics.

Remember this: Think before you take a laptop

Laptops can make the freelance travel writers life so much easier if you are able to write in your hotel room as this is a more profitable use of your time. However, as a luxury item, a laptop can draw attention/risk to you if you are travelling in remote, impoverished areas.

Subsidized travel

Freelance travel writers manage to minimize their travel expenses by getting the authorities at the destination and airlines/rail companies to provide travel in return for a full mention and contact details within the feature.

This is accepted practice but it does rely upon having a commission or proof of interest from an editor. If you find yourself in that happy position, then you are at liberty to contact airlines, train operators, tour operators, holiday companies and hotels that may be willing to provide you with their services for free or at a discount on the understanding that they will receive a mention in your feature.

Contact the tourist authorities and embassies of your destination and explain whom you are writing for and what you plan to write: they may well want details of the circulation figures and target audience of the intended publication, so make sure you have these facts to hand. Ask them if they can help you with accommodation, providing a guide or general information and assistance. Many of these organizations have budgets for just such ventures, and they can be extremely helpful and generous.

When I was writing for *Daily Mail Ski* magazine and *The Good Ski Guide,* the tour operators and the tourist authorities within the ski resorts were always helpful and usually very happy to contribute towards accommodation and travel in order to get their venue or company mentioned in these magazines.

If you are writing for a specialist publication, you should contact organizations involved in the promotion of the specialty in and around the destination. They may well be able to open doors that you could not on your own, and they may well offer some great hospitality while you are visiting, too. For example, if you are writing for a business title, then contact the equivalent of the Chamber of Commerce in the region. They will have contacts and advice for you at the very least.

You may wonder why these organizations might be so generous to a freelance travel writer but, in general, it is a good investment for them, as they know that freelancers have to sell their stories to several publications in order to maximize their earnings – in this way, they are getting wider coverage in return for their generosity.

Press trips

Once you have several pieces of published travel writing to your name, you can start to circulate your details to the travel public relations (PR) companies. They represent tour operators, travel companies and tourist authorities and often arrange educational trips for selected journalists to promote the services/destinations of their clients.

These are all-expenses-paid excursions and the scheduling and organization is done for you. You simply turn up and follow the itinerary. This limits the amount of freedom you have to pursue the more eccentric stories that might interest you, although, in my experience, PRs are very accommodating and will try to help you with your investigations, as long as it does not inconvenience the rest of the group of journalists.

I should sound a cautionary note while on the subject of press trips and subsidized travel. Just because you've been given hospitality and generosity on your trip, you still have a duty to write honestly about the destination. Clearly, tour operators, PRs, hotels and tourist authorities want you to write favourably about their product and will do their utmost to make sure your experience is a good one, but you cannot lie to the readers, and if you only write in glowing terms about everything, you will have difficulty selling the feature anyway – an editor can spot 'puff' at twenty paces.

The aim should be to find a balance. There might be something negative to say about the pollution in the streets of a Far Eastern city but this can be countered by something about the delights of the local cuisine. If you feel obliged to reveal something unpalatable about one aspect of a destination in a feature for one magazine, then an article on another aspect of the location might be glowing in a different title. If you are fair-handed in your reporting, you can usually hope to be asked back in the future.

Keep selling

Once you have got a commission from your first choice of publication, whether it is a consumer magazine, local paper or the trade press, then start to consider other outlets that might be interested in a travel feature. Travel writing is the most time-consuming genre of writing. In order to make it pay, you must ensure that time spent travelling plus time spent writing is recuperated in fees for articles/books. The only way for this to be workable is if you produce as much copy as possible from every trip. You are probably looking at in the region of four or five features per trip, depending on destination and duration, and of course rates of pay.

You cannot go to a direct competitor of your chosen publication (editors take a very dim view of such behaviour), so think about other media and think laterally. The main purpose of your trip may be to write about the condors of the Colca Canyon in Peru for a nature magazine, but if the Dakar rally happens to be passing close by while you are there, you could detour to cover this, interviewing drivers, team managers and locals alike, and then sell it to a motoring publication. What is the clubbing scene like in the major cities of Peru? Perhaps this could be of interest to a publication aimed at students or young travellers.

Always interview as many people as possible while travelling, even if it does not immediately seem clear how it might help the feature you are working on. An interview with leading businesspeople or political figures, interesting local characters, someone involved in charity work in the slums, or a European woman who has worked with local gangs – whatever it may be, with a little thought on your return, you might well be able to sell their story to a specialist publication. In fact, there are numerous stories in every region that you could sell to a range of different outlets – and don't forget online media, too.

NEW MEDIA

The explosion of blogs, online magazine and online communities means that there are more opportunities than ever for travel writers. Certainly at the start of your career, the new media arena probably represents the best opportunity for a would-be travel writer to get work out there.

Check out travel websites and subscribe to the outlet's newsletter or RSS feed so that you know precisely what they want, what they are currently purchasing and how to format it. You can then tailor your feature ideas to their goals.

You can start modestly on the social network sites such as Facebook, YouTube, Flickr, Travelistic, LinkedIn and Twitter, by putting up stories, photos and videos (having already edited out any indiscrete personal snaps) to show potential editors and to publicize your work. Alternatively, you could create a blog as a showcase for your writing talents, and link to your favourite travel sites – if they are impressed, they could well link back.

Once you have a portfolio of items, you could perhaps collect these together to form the basis of a travel book.

TRAVEL BOOKS

Travel books are rarely commissioned from anyone other than experienced travel writers or named celebrities. Nonetheless, if you have a number of themed articles or experiences, perhaps you could compile these into a travel book – there are lots of quirky titles on sale at the moment that centre around a central travel idea such as Tony Hawks' *Round Ireland with a Fridge*.

Key idea: Guidebook fees

The writer of the first edition of a guidebook should get a far higher fee than an updater. You should also be able to argue for first refusal on future updates. Picture research should be paid as an extra task.

Evoking a picture

Good travel writing should successfully bring the essence of a place to life for the reader. In order to do this, you need to provide sensual detail: What food did you eat? How did it taste and appear? What smells assaulted you? How did you feel? What were your first impressions? What did the place remind you of? From your hotel room, could you hear birdsong or the bustle of the local market? The aim is to appeal to the readers' senses so that they go on the journey with you.

Paradoxically, as well as your impressions of a destination, you also have to provide detail. So make sure you take copious notes when you are travelling as a writer rather than a tourist. A reader needs to come away with the necessary information to get about and to see the best sites, so: How much does it cost to get into an attraction. When is it busiest? How long has it been open? And so on. Ultimately, the reader should want to pack your book or tear out your article to take with them when they finish reading it; it should be helpful, accurate and honest if it is to be a good travel companion.

Just as you should have no qualms about telling the truth even if your trip is paid for, so there is no problem in having a point of view in travel writing. Your likes and dislikes can be legitimately shared with the reader so long as you can say why. In fact, a personal tone and your preferences can bring a piece of travel writing to life, as long as you remain accurate.

Try it now: Write a travel review

To evoke the sense of a place, you need to paint a sensual picture that appeals to all the senses. Try writing a review of your last holiday destination, bringing in descriptions of the taste of the food, the smells you remember, what images remain imprinted on your mind, how you felt, what sounds you woke up to... You get the gist. Remember to appeal to the readers' senses so they can journey with you.

Good photography sells

One of the most lucrative aspects of travel writing can be gained by investing in a good camera and perhaps taking a photographic course. You do not need a top-of-the-range SLR digital camera – a high-quality pocket digital camera will do – but if you can supply good-quality, high-resolution, interesting photographs, you can supplement your income from travel writing quite substantially, as publications will pay additionally for good photographs.

Remember this: Invest in a camera

It's worth investing in a good camera if you are serious about travel writing as you can increase your income significantly by selling good travel photos as well as your copy.

Bear in mind that photographs should relate specifically to the things that you talk about in your feature so, if you are selling different ideas to different outlets, then you need the full gamut of photographs. Provide captions along with the photographs to explain who or what they are of.

You can sell photographs to publications separately from selling features or as a package, generally commanding a higher price. Alternatively, you might like to consider selling your travel photographs to a photo library as a way of increasing your income from travel writing.

If you are submitting travel features to a website, then shoot some brief clips of video to accompany your words. Keep it brief, though – a minute of video is too long, as viewers have a very short attention span. A travel writer who can write well and provide good photos/video is definitely ahead of the game.

Try it now: Write a sample travel guide chapter

Write some sample text for a chapter of your travel guide, and then write some listings for the same destination, along the line of 'Best places to eat' or 'Top ten surfing locations', etc. You will discover that listings take far longer to write than running copy, so make sure that the publisher engages a fact-checker for your book. If you are required to check all listing information, you should charge an extra fee for this.

Case study: Tom Anderson, Travel Writer

Based in Porthcawl, South Wales, Tom Anderson is the author of the acclaimed travelogues Chasing Dean, Riding the Magic Carpet *and* Grey Skies Green Waves. *He also gives talks on travel writing in schools and at literary festivals.*

'While I was on the road travelling, I realized that this was the thing I enjoyed doing most in life (as well as surfing, which was what got me onto the road travelling in the first place). I thought well, I enjoy writing and, there must be other people like me out there, so why not write what would be my dream book? And the first book I wrote has sold about 10,000 copies now.

'I think that nowadays, with the amount of travelling writing, it's essential to have a specialism. Jonathan Rayban, my favourite travel writer, talks about travel writing having to have some kind of purpose and that you have to strike a balance between a self-indulgent personal journey that no one can identify with that leaves you with an aimless wandering narrative and something that's excessively ingenious and becomes very limiting and a little too quirky.

'I've just finished reading a fantastic travel book, *Cloud Road* by Welshman John Harrison, which won the Welsh Travel Book of the Year 2011. In that book, he travels through the Andes on foot and intersperses his own personal journey with an historical account of the conquest of the Andes by the Spaniards. You get a story going along which gives him a purpose for being there.

'In that book he talks about the problem of books like the *Lonely Planet* guides which have basically given every country in the world an itinerary that everyone follows so you're on a kind of carousel. In my case, surfing certainly gets you off that carousel... and off the beaten track. If you go chasing the surf break, you can find yourself in little villages away from the main tourist area. Surfing gives you a purpose for being there. It also means that a lot of the people you meet are all sharing that common purpose as well. I think it also allows you to make connections with people. It's something that transcends barriers of language and cultural background if everyone's after the same thing.

'My tip to would-be travel writers is that it's absolutely essential that you can talk. I make as much money from giving after-dinner talks as I do from book royalties. I'm also a qualified teacher so I go into schools and talk about being a travel writer. I go on the radio... BBC Wales will phone me if there's anything on surfing or travel in the news and they usually pay about £30 for that. So, I usually pick up a fair income – a couple of thousand pounds a year – from talking and doing other related things.

'As part of a talk in schools I get them to produce their own piece of travel writing in about 1½ hours. Kids just really like that and I get sponsored by the Welsh Literature Council and, as part of their Writers on Tour Scheme, they pay half the fees that the writer charges back to the school. I get a lot of business through that.

'The Hay Festival and things like that are good, although Hay isn't paid – you get a yellow rose and a bottle of champagne for doing it but it generates a profile; I'd like to think I've got a reasonable profile, so I get booked to talk. Being able to talk about what you do is really important if you want to make money from travel writing.'

Focus points

The main points to remember from this chapter are:

* ✴ Do your background research on a destination before you go.
* ✴ Choose less familiar locations or come up with a different angle for the more popular places.
* ✴ Look at ways to get your trip subsidized or paid for.
* ✴ For every trip you take, make sure there are several outlets for features to maximize earnings.
* ✴ Good travel writing should be a mix of acute observation, striking description and detailed information, all in your own personal style.

Next step

You've learned in this chapter about bringing a place to life by description that appeals to the senses. In Chapter 8, we'll look at ways to earn money from successfully writing for the spoken word, which includes broadcast media such as radio and television as well as podcasts.

8

Writing for broadcasting

In this chapter you will learn:

▸ *That radio can be a good starting place for many freelance writers who want to work in the media*

▸ *That all broadcast media demand a concise and punchy writing style*

▸ *That the trustworthiness of your material is key in the media*

▸ *That podcasts provide exciting and expanding new opportunities for the freelance writer.*

Assessment: Evaluate your suitability for writing for the broadcast media

Your answers to the following questionnaire may well reveal your suitability to writing for the broadcast media:

1 Are you able to come up with lots of ideas for features, interviews and/or podcasts?

        YES   NO   PROBABLY (with practice)

2 Do you like researching background information to include in your features?

        YES   NO   PROBABLY (with practice)

3 Are you comfortable interviewing and empathizing with people?

        YES   NO   PROBABLY (with practice)

4 Can you write succinctly and to a prescribed length (duration of broadcast item)?

        YES   NO   PROBABLY (with practice)

5 Are you comfortable with the sound of your own voice?

        YES   NO   PROBABLY (with practice)

6 Are you confident in front of a camera?

        YES   NO   PROBABLY (with practice)

7 Can you communicate effectively, clearly and concisely?

        YES   NO   PROBABLY (with practice)

8 Do you have specialist knowledge or experience that people would be willing to pay for?

        YES   NO   PROBABLY (with practice)

9 Do you have the confidence to pitch your ideas to a producer?

        YES   NO   PROBABLY (with practice)

10 Are you good with technology?

        YES   NO   PROBABLY (with practice)

Scoring: Give yourself 2 points for each question to which you answered 'Yes'. Give yourself 1 point if you answered 'Probably (with practice)' and 0 points for all 'No' answers.

Assessment: If your score is:

15–20 points: Broadcast media seems to be an ideal vehicle for your specific talents. Read on to find out which branch of the genre best suits you.

8–14 points: There are certain aspects of writing for broadcasting that you are going to have to work on if you want to break into this competitive arena. However, with practice this goal should be achievable.

0–7 points: Depending on the questions that let you down, it may be that you'd be better as a backroom writer rather than a presenter, or you may simply prefer a medium where the pressures and deadlines are not so acute and there is less of a sense of immediacy.

Although broadcast media is still a competitive market, the good news for those wanting to write for radio and television is the insatiable demand for new material. If you think about the number of radio stations and televisions channels broadcasting 24 hours a day, seven days a week, then you will have some notion of the quantity of writing required. And this can only be a good thing for freelancers, even those without previous experience.

The skills needed for the broadcast media are different from those used by a print journalist, but it is merely an adaptation of style rather than a whole new skills set. For example, writing for the spoken word requires that you write to time constraints rather than word counts but it's a very similar discipline. So, if you were writing a script for a documentary, you must be able to tell the story in the right number of words to fit into the few seconds that a particular image is on the screen. News items, plays, even advertisements must be timed to the second.

Writing for radio

There are various outlets for a freelance writer for radio. These are:

- ▶ Creating scripts
- ▶ Reporting news items
- ▶ Writing commentary (opinion or insight features).

The good news is that there are still budgets available for buying material from freelancers in radio and, because it is not quite so glamorous as its televisual cousin, it is not quite so competitive either. Scriptwriting is probably the hardest genre to crack, but if you identify a radio slot that your work would fit into, you can always find out who is producing it and contact them to see if they would consider a script.

Many comedy and quiz projects start out on radio and, if they prove popular, they then make the transition to television. You could send a few gags to a comedian via his/her agent (for which you get paid if they use them) and, if they like your material, it could lead to creating more material with that comedian in mind, either for radio or television.

But the most likely outlet for a novice writer is in the field of commentary or news.

WRITING STYLE

You have to be extremely concise in your style when writing for the radio. If you consider that a feature for the print media can run to several thousand words, for the radio, you'll be lucky if a commentary runs to 700 words, and a news story barely scrapes 100 words.

Remember this: Keep it brief!

A radio news story usually runs for around 20 to 30 seconds. As a rough guideline, you can work on a rate of approximately 155 words per minute for the spoken word. When counting up the length of your script, numerals and symbols each count as one word; so your average news item is only around 77 words long – that's not much to play with, so make sure you are concise.

Here are a few more style tips:

▶ Use language that you might hear in everyday speech (without becoming too informal) and appropriate for the listenership.

▶ Use the present or present continuous tense, even if an event has already happened, to keep immediacy, e.g. 'UK Energy Secretary quits [or is quitting] over criminal charges.'

▶ Keep sentences simple and avoid compound or complex sentences and relative clauses wherever possible.

▶ Avoid the passive voice and using 'there is' or 'there are', as these sentence structures use up valuable words. For example change 'There is a large compensation package of £15,000 being offered to all employees who have been affected by the gas leak' to 'A £15,000 compensation package is on offer to all gas-affected employees.'

▶ Keep it easy to read out, so write exactly what you want the listener to hear. To that effect, spell out all symbols, so £100 becomes 'one hundred pounds' and numerals are written in full, e.g. 'Call oh-eight-hundred-six-eight-six-eight.'

▶ You might be familiar with local names or specialist terminology but the presenter reading out your script may not, so include the phonetic pronunciation of difficult words and unusual names at the end of the item to ensure they are read out correctly.

Try it now: Read your script out loud

Before submitting your script, read it out loud. You may feel silly but it's the best way to make sure the language is comprehensible and sounds natural, and to make sure there are no typing or grammatical gaffes. Bizarrely, you are more likely to pick these up when reading out loud as the eye skims over them when reading silently.

SUBMISSIONS

If you are going to pitch an idea to a radio producer or news editor, send an email, keeping the pitch brief. Simply outline the salient points of the story and why you think it would be great for this particular station. If there is a tantalizing hook, so much the better.

At this stage, there is no need to send in audio. If the station likes your pitch, it will contact you and, in the case of news, either send you out with professional gear to get the story or ask you to send the text and possibly an audio clip, usually as an MP3 file.

If they like your style, who knows, they might start to commission work from you more regularly.

Key idea: Spoilt for choice

There are 40 BBC local radio stations and more than 250 commercial stations (known as ILR – Independent Local Radio stations) in the UK, so there are plenty of outlets for your submissions. Nonetheless, if you find yourself getting constant rejections owing to lack of experience, you could volunteer at your local hospital or community radio station. You won't get paid but you will get your expenses and necessary experience.

Writing for television

There are a few well-known names who write for television but it is a notoriously hard field to break into despite the voracious demand for new material. Many writers cut their teeth in radio, and then, once they are established, transfer across to television.

Try it now: Watch and learn

Make sure you listen to or watch any show that you are about to pitch to. If you go in blind, a producer will spot your lack of research immediately. So listen, watch and learn.

You are unlikely to make any money supplying news stories to television as the 'stringers' (freelancers) used are almost always ex-staffers. However, there are plenty of other outlets for fiction and non-fiction writers and you can try as many as you like. Whether it's a script for a period drama or soap, a pilot for a sitcom, sketches for a comedy show or a documentary, you could send in some samples of your work to the producers, and you may end up working alongside the established writers on the team.

WRITING STYLE

Whatever you are writing for television, there are a few concepts to keep in mind if you are to stand any chance of selling your idea:

▶ Subject is king – there has to be an interested audience.

▶ Think visually – will your story work as images?

▶ Be responsible – powerful TV can inspire a change in attitudes, both socially and personally, so think carefully about the message you are conveying.

▶ Credibility – your sources and research must be reliable. A producer will never use you again if they get complaints that your work was inaccurate.

SUBMISSIONS

Just as with radio, it is customary to email a television production company or producer with an outline of your idea, which you can then discuss in more detail with them if they show signs of interest.

However, as in all other cases, the unproven writer may need to send the finished article as you will not be considered without a track record. So, make sure you are sending your work in the conventional format. You can find examples of scripts for television shows and their layout at www.bbc.co.uk/writersroom and www.simplyscripts.com

You can also buy specialized software for scriptwriting, which makes life so much easier. Examples include Final Draft or Microsoft's Screenplay Template (free to Microsoft Word users) or Scriptsmart (Microsoft Word templates and macros for formatting scripts), which can be found at the BBC Writersroom site.

Your target production company may well issue guidelines on submissions, so check out their websites before you contact them.

Try it now: Set yourself a tough deadline

Independent film and TV companies use freelance writers but they work to tight deadlines. They sometimes send out documentary tapes in the morning expecting to have the completed script back that evening. So try setting yourself a tough writing deadline and make sure you meet it. Practice makes perfect.

Podcasts

Although podcasting has been around less than a decade, in this technological age, you cannot fail to have heard a podcast. It is a mini radio show that you record and put on the Internet for download onto iPods or other MP3 players. Still not sure? Well, check out websites such as YouTube and iTunes and there are countless podcasts for you to sample.

There is no such thing as a typical podcast because there is such a wide spectrum of content in this field. Nonetheless, a podcast normally lasts in the region of 15 minutes to an hour, and it can be on any subject under the sun, as long as you do not infringe copyright laws. You can post a podcast as frequently as you like and the vast majority are free, although occasionally you are asked to pay a subscription.

Not only are podcasts a great way to practise your writing because they have to be scripted, but, just like blogs, you may attract a following. There are other ways that you can make money from a popular podcast.

Remember this: Script every podcast

Podcasts of around 15 to 20 minutes are most successful, as you don't want to bore your listeners by waffling on for hours. Keep the content tight and to the point, and to avoid umming and aahing, make sure you script each podcast.

MAKING MONEY FROM PODCASTING

In order to make money, you have to have a subject that you know a great deal about or that you love talking about. But more importantly, you have to offer your listener something unique and useful that they cannot get elsewhere for free. If you satisfy these basic criteria, then you might be able to convert this knowledge into cash.

You can sell your content by charging a small payment for each downloaded podcast. Companies such as PayPal or the Amazon Honour System help you to collect payments for digital content from your users, and you pay only a small percentage to them. You can perhaps release your podcasts in a programme – say once or twice a week – and if your content offers good information that people cannot get elsewhere, then they will be willing to pay.

Perhaps you do not have specialist knowledge that you can sell. Perhaps your podcast attracts a large following because it is well scripted and informative or entertaining. Whatever the reason, if it's popular, you can sell ads that run within your podcast. Businesses are always looking for ways to reach new customers, and if your podcast connects with their ideal target audience, you can make extra money this way. Of course, you will have to be able to show them how many listeners and/or subscribers you reach in order to persuade them. If you do not have the time or the inclination to approach businesses yourself in order to sell ads, then you could join a podcast ad network.

A creative twist on the direct advertising idea is to find and promote a sponsor on your podcast. Especially if you are in a niche market, you can approach a company for sponsorship in return for promoting that company in your weekly podcast.

Of course, if you have your own product to promote, you can use your podcast to sell it. For a writer, a podcast can be a good way to sell your ebook for example. Alternatively, you can make money from selling other people's products by using an affiliate programme, where you make a commission or earn a fixed payment when someone buys something that you linked them to. For example, if you want to sell other people's ebooks, you could go to www.clickbank.com, but other affiliate sites include Amazon, ShareASale and Commission Junction. Just one word of caution, it's always worth checking out the quality/authenticity of any product you sell through your podcast, as you do not want to alienate your listeners in any way.

Finally, make sure that, if you sell anything directly through your site, you collect their details for your mailing list, so they can get your podzine newsletter. Invest in email marketing software such as AWeber, which is easy to use and inexpensive. Unlike your podcast, a monthly podzine can carry links to products and services that you recommend. And, if there is an affiliate programme for that product, you can get paid for any sales that originate from your podzine.

Try it now: Keep abreast of new developments

Keep abreast of developments in the field by signing up for free newsletters on technical and new media-oriented websites.

Case study: Ben Ransom, Producer at Sky Sports News Radio

'What I'm looking for in a freelancer is quite simple really. They've got to be able to write. They've got to be able to write for radio and they've got to know exactly what the top line is. I have people approach me from different backgrounds, both from journalism and non-journalism, and they tell me they are interested in sport and can write. So the first thing I do is to ask them for a quick copy story or package, and you can see straight away whether they've got the top line right. The key to writing for radio is that everything is "tight and bright".

'In radio every second is valuable, it's precious, so the script has to be tight – you can't throw away any words or phrases, you have to say things as succinctly as possible. If you give someone a huge waffling piece of copy and they can turn that into three or four lines that captures the essence of the story with a strong top line, it's going to make you want to listen. Quite simply, if it makes you want to listen, it's a good bit of writing.

'For radio, you have to showcase your talents. You can imagine how many submissions come through the door with people just sending their CV and saying I want to come and do this for you. It's essential that you demonstrate a knowledge of the station and its audience, because every single radio station has a very specific demographic that they aim at. If you show an understanding of who that audience is, then you can pitch stories and news that automatically interests that audience. That's the sort of thing we look for.

'It's important that you tailor every pitch. For example, you wouldn't offer an in-depth expose about the financial crisis in world football to a commercial radio station. It simply wouldn't fit in with their entertainment-based output. It's the sort of story you might instead pitch to Sky Sports News Radio or BBC Radio Five Live. You would need to find a station whose listeners go to that specific brand for such a product.

'Work placements for radio are invaluable. You have to prove to an employer that you can deliver in a work environment. There are so many people who want to write or broadcast on the radio, TV or even on the Internet. With such high-quality training courses available, lots of people also have the skills to do just that, so it's about making yourself stand out from the crowd. Specialism can be helpful for this. You need to offer an employer something that they don't already have.

'I started out as a news journalist when I graduated with a Master's in Broadcast Journalism. Although I have an interest in current affairs, my real passion is sport – and I think it's instantly recognizable from my work. It's a mistake to look at the two subjects as mutually exclusive; some of the biggest news stories of recent years have been from the world of sport. But when you have a passion for a particular subject, like sport, it enables you to come up with stronger news angles to interest your listeners that other stations might not pick up on. After all, we're all fighting for a share of the market!

'When you're getting started it's about meeting as many people as you can. It's about going into the newsroom itself with confidence and the right attitude. Arm yourself with the essential knowledge to succeed in that environment – understand what the product is, who the audience is and whom exactly you're writing for. With everything you do, go through a mental checklist – Is it interesting to me? Is it interesting to the audience? Has it got a strong top line? If the answer to all of those questions is "yes", then more often than not it will work.

'Initially, it's not worth investing in expensive equipment as you need to be guaranteed the work to pay it off. I would never suggest anyone spends £500 on a recorder if they're never going to get to use it. I think the way to do it is go in to a newsroom, show you've got something about you and prove you can do it. Further down the line, you're getting regular work and people are saying, 'This person is really good, but he or she would be more useful if they had their own recording equipment,' then it's something to look at. But often, if you're getting on well at a radio station and making a contribution, the equipment will be there for you to borrow – that's certainly been my experience.

'You might get the impression that the radio landscape is bleak, with newsrooms shrinking and fewer permanent positions for journalists. But in a funny way it has actually led to openings in the broadcast media, particularly for freelance employees. Stations are still relying on generating the same output despite having fewer employees. Often the burden falls on contracted staff to do more work, but we can't be there all the time. Suddenly, you're left with a newsroom with half the number of staff – and you've still got to fill the same amount of hours. You need people who can come in and do a decent job for a day, a week or month here and there. If you can prove you can be flexible, fill gaps and be reliable then openings can present themselves. Everyone is looking to save money and time, so if a writer is not necessarily looking for a full-time contract but is looking to get involved in the industry, the opportunities are there.'

Focus points

The main points to remember from this chapter are:

* Radio offers a great platform for novice writers, so experiment with different genres within the field.
* Be prepared to invest in recording equipment if you are going to pursue this as a career (though not at the outset).

* Television is hard to break into, but once you've identified the programme-makers that are producing the sort of shows you want to be part of, you can write something that will show them what you are capable of.
* Podcasts are a great way to broadcast your specialist knowledge and there are spin-offs such as advertising that can earn revenue.
* Practise the writing style for broadcast media – tight, pertinent and punchy.

Next step

The writing skills required for the broadcast media, namely a succinct, easily comprehensible style, are very similar to those used in the expanding field of new media. Why not use these transferable skills to increase your potential earnings and get into this new and exciting field, as will be discussed in Chapter 9?

9

Writing for new media

In this chapter you will learn:

- ▶ *How to set up a blog*
- ▶ *How blogs can be used as a promotional tool for other outlets – e.g. to publicize a book/ebook*
- ▶ *How blogs can also generate income in other ways*
- ▶ *About the expanding market for ebooks*
- ▶ *About the advantages and disadvantages of self-publishing.*

Assessment: Evaluate your suitability for writing for new media

Answer the following questionnaire to find out whether or not you are well suited to writing for new media:

1 Are you technologically minded?

> YES   NO

2 Do you have time to monitor blogs etc. on a daily basis?

> YES   NO

3 Can you write succinct, entertaining and engaging copy?

> YES   NO

4 Do you enjoy using social media such as Facebook, Twitter, YouTube, etc.?

> YES   NO

5 Do you have contacts with websites that could link to you?

> YES   NO

6 Do you have a way of marketing yourself to your audience?

> YES   NO

7 Do you have funds available to invest in and maintain new media technology?

> YES   NO

8 Do you have a reputation in an area of specialization or expertise?

> YES   NO

9 Do you have something to offer your readers other than views and/or entertainment?

> YES   NO

10 Do you have any design or creative experience?

> YES   NO

In recent years, a media revolution has taken place and we now have an astonishing choice regarding how and when we consume the news and media. Developments in IT and printing technology mean that, via a range of new media including blogging, ebooks and self-publishing, writers are able to reach a global audience with relative ease. This has created new openings for those wishing to make money from writing. Having said that, don't be lulled into thinking this is a way to make a fast buck – to be a professional blogger or self-publisher requires dedication, investment and hard work.

Blogging

It is said that a new blog is launched every second. A blog (a newly coined word that is a blend of 'Web' and 'log') is most commonly used as a kind of online diary. Yet, it is not the sole preserve of those who wish to share their idle musings or impart their philosophies and views to the world. There is a growing band of writers and business-savvy pioneers who are turning a blog into a money-maker. For those who are already freelance writers, whether selling articles, books or writing for business, running a couple of niche blogs is proving to be a good way to augment their income.

If your blog becomes well known within a particular niche, you can always sell advertising space on your site. There are services such as Google's AdSense which allow you to select several ads that are in keeping with your blog's content and you get paid on how many readers click on the ads for further information. Alternatively, services such as BlogAds connect bloggers with potential advertisers and then take a commission in return for any ad placements that result.

Key idea: Keep a blog

In the current climate, publishers want new authors to have a platform. A blog is a great platform for a writer because it allows you to communicate your message over time to an expanding fan-base and it also allows you to capture email addresses using a service like Feedburner or AWeber.

SETTING UP A BLOG

For the non-techno among us, there are sites such as blogger.com which offer free blogging. They are easy to use and to personalize and you are given your own address to give to friends and clients who may want to take a look. Once you have chosen your host site, you simply enter your details to create an account, and then you are free to upload your data and/or photos or videos. When you are happy with what you have created, hit 'publish' and your words are live for all to see.

Alternatively, if you want to buy your own domain name (website) and host it, which might be advisable if you have a niche market, then you can go to sites such as Bluehost, Yahoo! Web Hosting or HostGator and use their search facility to see if your chosen name is available. If it is, you can then open an account, and buy the domain and hosting from them (a two-year hosting package costs about £120 but there are other durations available as well as unlimited hosting packages).

Now you have your site, there are dozens of platforms such as WordPress for installing and managing blogs. The customer services department of your hosting company will be happy to help you with the process, which should take less than an hour.

WRITING A BLOG

If anyone is going to read your blog, it has to have some real content. What you have to say should be entertaining and/ or informative. Writing style for the Internet is different from writing for print media – make sure you keep your sentences short and punchy and the information succinct, as it's hard to read large chunks of text on a computer screen.

The keywords that you choose need to appear frequently in the content of your blog's article – tags go on the post and are used as anchor text to create incoming links. This may all sound baffling to the uninitiated but, once you start your blog, it will all become clear.

Incoming links from other websites to your blog are just one indicator that search engines use when deciding on prominence given to sites. So link building is vital. Ask friends or colleagues with sites that you link to or recommend to reciprocate wherever possible. You can also increase traffic by commenting on other people's blogs. Several blogging or article sites (Blogger, Hubpages, Ezine articles and WordPress to mention but a few) also allow you to post articles containing links to your own sites.

Keep your blog regularly updated with lively, well-expressed ideas and word will soon spread as friends tell others. As word gets around, so you will find readers leave feedback and comments and these discussions can be a useful source of ideas and direction.

Finally, don't be afraid to have an opinion or to share knowledge. This is your platform and it can reflect your personality, views and opinions (as long as they are not litigious) as well as showcase your knowledge and writing talents.

Try it now: Attract traffic to your site

In order to make money from a blog you need people to be aware of your site, and for that to happen you must be highly visible to the search engines. So before launching your niche blog, you should research the competition and possible search terms for attracting traffic to your site. Give it a go, but if you are out of your depth, there are excellent services with instructional videos in this field, such as Market Samurai. Its product costs around £95 (although there are also free downloadable trials available), though most professional bloggers believe this is money well invested.

Key idea: Blooks

Books that are spawned by blogs have created a new word, 'blooks'. There is even a Blooker Prize. All right, it's not common but it happens – in 2006, more than 100 bloggers landed book deals in the US. Not convinced? Just consider chart-topping book and box-office hit film *Julie and Julia* by Julie Powell, which started life as a blog when she decided to document her attempts to work her way through all the recipes in Julia Child's 1961 recipe book.

Ebooks

With the growing sophistication of mobile phones and handheld ebook readers such as the iPad and Kindle, there has been a boom in the number of ebooks available. America led the charge, where in 2009 ebooks made up 15 per cent of overall books sales, but the sales of ebooks is rising at an exponential rate in the UK, too. Part of the appeal is the versatility of ebooks – you can buy and download a whole book or you can pay for it chapter by chapter.

So how can a writer make money from ebooks? Certainly, it is easy enough to produce an ebook. If you are techno-savvy you can use publishing software to produce your ebook on your own website. You are then free to sell it through your website by setting up a merchant account with your bank or by using a third-party merchant such as PayPal which takes a small transaction fee. These payment options are relatively easy to install, and, once set up, virtually all of the profits from your ebook are paid directly to you.

Alternatively, you could approach an e-publisher and there are many to choose from. For example, with an e-publisher such as e-junkie.com, you pay about $5 (roughly £3.15) per month, for unlimited download bandwidth for ebooks, although they have a 50 MB storage limit. If you use a company such as PayPal or Google CheckOut to process the money and credit card orders for your sales, you will end up earning about 90 per cent of the cover price of your ebook.

Not to be sniffed at. However, if no one knows about your website, you are not going to sell any books and you'll be earning 90 per cent of nothing. So, the truth is that you can earn a substantially bigger proportion of the cover price of your book than if you went through a traditional print publisher, but you must have a platform to reach a wide audience if this is to be profitable. Without a client base, platform or other route to the paying public, ebooks are not going to make you money.

It should also be borne in mind that ebooks tend to sell for a much lower price than their traditional hardback equivalent. For example, *The Etymologicon* by Mark Forsyth was a publishing sensation at Christmas 2011, but whereas it sold for £12.99 at Waterstones, it cost just 99p as a Kindle ebook. So you are getting 90 per cent of income, say, but it is 90 per cent of less than a pound.

Self-publishing and print on demand

Instead of using the traditional route to publication through an established publishing house, more and more writers are taking matters into their own hands and deciding to publish their books through self-publishing and print on demand publishing.

For those with ready access to a paying audience, this can be a sensible and profitable decision. However, if you have no way to market you book or to reach your target audience after publication, this can be a costly business and you could lose every penny that you invest in the venture.

Effectively, with this option, you bear all the costs up front, as you do not have an advance from a publisher. These costs can soon mount up and could include design, editing and proofreading services as well as the major cost of printing. Print costs are lower per book the more you have printed. However, you must be honest in your predictions of how many copies you can sell. If you are left with several thousand copies, even if the original unit price was lower, you are going to be substantially out of pocket. Plus you have the additional headache of storing the unsold copies.

On a happier note, if you have access to a large database, perhaps because you run workshops/courses/classes or you have specialist knowledge and access to the associated specialist networks (for example, the MG Midget fan club, or a small specialist business with a devoted clientele), then you can potentially sell a lot of books through these outlets. And you stand to make considerably more money from each sale than if you were published via the traditional route because you earn the publisher's share of the profits as well.

In addition, with your book in print, you have a product and sales figures to show to a potential publisher and, if the product and sales are sufficiently impressive, this is a persuasive argument for getting into a mainstream publishing house.

 Remember this: Steer clear of the 'vanity press'

There is a big difference between self-publishing and what's known as vanity publishing, which is to be avoided. The vanity press, who variously advertise their services as 'subsidy publishing', 'joint venture publishing' or even 'co-contributing publishing partners', exploit the naive and the desperate. They will ask for money towards cost and will always give an unrealistically high prediction on sales figures. You have been warned.

CHOOSING THE RIGHT SERVICE

There are companies who specialize in offering self-publishing packages to the would-be writer. You can choose from a full spectrum of services, ranging from the complete package or just the selected services you want. Shop around, as fees can vary substantially, and make sure you know exactly what you're getting in return for your money.

Realistically, you are probably looking at an initial print run of between 500 and 1,000 copies of your book. With such modest figures, the printing and binding costs can work out quite expensive per copy, so make sure you reflect this in your price to the customer.

With print on demand (POD) or available on demand (AOD) publishing, you can order as many or as few copies of your book as you want because it is digitally printed rather than produced on a printing press, as in conventional publishing. Nonetheless, this does not solve the problem of needing to have a way to market your book and, as with self-publishing, there is no after-sales support as you would get with a traditional publisher.

Even so, many mainstream publishers now have POD services which they use for books that only sell a handful of copies each year but that the publisher wants to keep on their list. And this is where POD can be profitable for an author, too. If your book has not sold well for a publisher and has not earned out its advance, they may well decide not to retain the rights when these come up for renewal. If the rights revert to you, reproducing your book by POD or as an ebook (the layout may have to be changed as publisher's copyright in 'the typographical arrangement of the published edition' lasts 25 years) can be a good way to make money from the product if you can find a new audience.

Just a final word of caution, if you go down the ebook, self-publishing or POD route, I suggest you check the contract very carefully. In fact, I recommend that you get the contract checked out by the Society of Authors or a lawyer specializing in publishing contracts, as there can be clauses within it that might tie you in to royalty payments to the printing company.

Case study: Elizabeth King, Blogger and Author of *Water Birth Please*

'I first got interested in writing a blog when I had my daughter two years ago. At that time, a very good friend of mine had been doing a blog for about a year, and she showed me what was involved. I thought it was a lovely way to log what being a new mum was about, and being a bit of a technophobe, I saw it more as keeping a diary online rather than getting into the technicalities of setting up a website, even though essentially that's what it is.

'To set up, I used a forum called WordPress, which is exceptionally user-friendly and free as well. But there's another one called Blogger, which is very popular, and iPad has just set up its own version, too. It's getting more and more user-friendly. I had my friend to sit and guide me through the initial stages and I've since done that for other people.

'I wanted to write about my daughter – it's easy to write about the things that you love and that you're enthusiastic about. Generally, people set their blogs up out of love or interest – I don't think you could write a blog about something you're not interested in.

'I also wanted to write as a way of helping me through losing my mum. I'd been down other roads that weren't for me, such as counselling, but I actually found the writing ten times more beneficial than anything else on offer.

'It amazes me still when I look back at some of the comments you get – sometimes it takes a stranger to touch you the most deeply really. There were women I found on line – new mums who had been through exactly the same thing as me, which you very rarely find in day-to-day life. There's a tremendous amount of support to be found from this little online community that I never knew existed.

'I just literally saw it as a hobby and something to show my daughter when she was older. Yet, things have come along that I wasn't expecting. I've made online friends. It's led to product reviews, which are really good fun, such as toy testing and things like that. They approached me but you can also join various media sites that will hook up suitable bloggers and manufacturers who want their products reviewed.

'Also an ebook has come about because of the blog. It got to the point where I thought I could do a bit more with this. So I Googled online publishers and sent off a plethora of emails with an attachment to my blog, saying, "What do you think?" Out of that, one got back to me saying,

"We really like the style of your humour and we think it could do quite well." They wanted to take the more humorous posts and edit them so it read like a six-month diary in the life of a manic mum. They were fantastically supportive. They talked me through the whole process. Then my book was there. It's the best feeling in the world.

'My book is called *Water Birth Please* – it's an ironic take on my beautiful holistic birth-plan that I had and which went out of the window. The blog and the book have the same name so that they work together – the publishers advised me that the two could bounce off each other.

'You can view your statistics and find out who's viewing the blog and how many people. A lot of people get quite hung up on statistics and quite competitive about it, but I try not to. However, I think a lot of people have been led to the book through the blog.

'I'd love to do more writing. I really feel I've found an outlet and I love doing it. The book lends itself to a volume 2 and I've had some requests for a second one. One of the nicest compliments I got paid was from a heavily pregnant lady with her third child who was having a very down time – she was very fed up. She said she downloaded my book and that she was laughing out loud. It completely cheered her up. And I thought what a lovely compliment – to affect someone like that whom you had never met.

'It's not about making tons of money; it's about a sense of achievement really. And I make a bit of money and it's a nice legacy for my daughter.'

www.waterbirthplease.wordpress.com

Focus points

The main points to remember from this chapter are:

* New media can instantly create a rapport and dialogue between you and your audience and offers immediacy.
* Ebooks can seriously increase your revenue from book sales if you have a route to market.
* A good website or blog can be a showcase for your talents.
* On-demand publishing gives you a finished product that can help to market your skills.
* There are writers who earn a living from blogging, but it usually requires more than one site.

Next step

If marketing your own writing services through new media is something that comes naturally to you, perhaps you should consider using your skills to market other people and their products/services. The next chapter on writing for PR or directly for corporate clients will show you ways to earn money from writing for business.

10

Writing for business

In this chapter you will learn:

▶ *About the massive range of opportunities available to writers in the business world*

▶ *How freelance fees for freelance business writers are usually a lot higher than for writers working for the traditional media*

▶ *How to build a portfolio for business and sell your services.*

Assessment: Evaluate your suitability for writing commercial copy

How you answer the following questions will give you some idea of your suitability for writing commercial copy:

1 Do you have good communications skills?

YES NO PROBABLY (with practice)

2 Are you able to write to a brief?

YES NO PROBABLY (with practice)

3 Do you like researching subjects?

YES NO PROBABLY (with practice)

4 Are you comfortable interviewing people?

YES NO PROBABLY (with practice)

5 Can you take what a specialist is saying and put it into a language that is comprehensible and interesting to others?

YES NO PROBABLY (with practice)

6 Can you adjust your style for different types and styles of firms and corporate literature?

YES NO PROBABLY (with practice)

7 Can you mix comfortably with people from a different background/working environment to your own?

YES NO PROBABLY (with practice)

8 Can you promote and sell yourself?

YES NO PROBABLY (with practice)

9 Do you have a specialism or area of interest so that you could focus on firms in this arena?

YES NO PROBABLY (with practice)

10 Do you have contacts in the corporate or PR world?

YES NO PROBABLY (with practice)

Once you get into the field of writing for the business community, it is one of the more lucrative ways to earn money from your craft. But, like many of the other genres of writing, beginners often find themselves in a catch-22 situation: until you have a portfolio of work, no one will employ you; and you cannot get a portfolio until someone gives you work.

Clearly, if you are already writing in another field, this conundrum is partially solved for you, as you have published work to show a prospective employer, albeit that it may be in an unrelated field.

For those new to the business, you are going to have to be bold and to use any contacts you might have. For many, that means that your first business writing ventures may have to be viewed as a loss-leader.

Get in touch with all of your contacts in the business world and tell them that you will write some promotional material for their business free of charge – they only have to bear the production costs, which they would probably be spending in any event. If it's a press release, these are almost always sent out by email, so there is no cost to the business owner in any event.

Remember this: Volunteer to write for your company newsletter

If writing is just an aspiration or a way to supplement an income from full-time employment in another field, you could get some published work by volunteering to contribute to your company newsletter (or to start one if your firm doesn't already have one). It is good writing experience and it's something to put in your portfolio.

Once you have some published work under your belt and a few corporate names you can mention as being ongoing clients, you are in a position to start approaching other businesses and charging for your services.

Try it now: Build a portfolio

If you have no portfolio and no personal contacts to approach in the corporate or PR world, why not contact small charities and other organizations in the voluntary sector and offer your writing services for free? It may give you the writing experience and portfolio you need so you can go on to approach paying clients.

Why businesses need writers

One of the reasons that writing for the business world can be such an attractive financial proposition is that there are so many different outlets to choose from. As well as the countless businesses who need a specialist to help them to communicate with their clients and their employees, there are also openings for a writer in the forms of press releases, brochures, company magazines and histories, in-house magazines, training material, conference material, report writing... the list is endless.

Surprising as it may be to you as a writer, most other people actually find writing a daunting prospect at best and terrifying at worst. If the firm is not large enough to have a marketing or PR team, they may well be very happy to pay for the services of a professional writer, just as they would pay for the specialist skills of a recruitment agency when looking for new staff or a catering firm when hosting a luncheon. This leaves them free to get on with what they are good at and they get a product that they can be proud of.

If they use in-house staff to write, there is always the danger that the person is so close to the business that they cannot ask the right questions or that they cannot communicate the necessary information in a way that is easily understandable to their target audience. They may well use language that excludes those outside the trade and that is full of jargon and unintelligible acronyms that they no longer 'see'. Your job is to ask the right questions and to interpret the answers in a manner that is accessible to the layperson.

Selling your services

Here you have to be bold. There is no point in hiding your light under a bushel – if you want to be paid for your writing services, then you are effectively selling yourself and your skills to a business. First and foremost, you should identify which market sectors are relevant to your experience, specialities (if any) and interests. These are the firms to target first.

Exploit any specialism you may have. Your early days writing for a trade magazine on plumbing supplies may not have been your most exciting, but you can use the specialist knowledge you acquired to approach kitchen and bathroom manufacturers, and that could lead you on to interior designers and the DIY market, or even commercial property consultants. All have corporate literature and employee communications and all welcome specialist writers.

In a small to medium-sized business, you can contact the owner, managing director or marketing director (usually bigger businesses) directly.

Send them an email or letter that:

▶ introduces you and your particular strengths, e.g. an ability to explain specialist topics in layman's terms

▶ explains the services you can provide, such as writing press releases and promotional material

- outlines how your services might benefit this particular company

- points out that you have enclosed some samples of your work (not too many – you can always offer them more if you get a bite or direct them to your website where all your work is on display).

Be prepared to follow up this initial approach with a phone call where you can expand on the services and benefits that you offer. While you are on the phone, you will almost certainly be asked about fees, so be prepared (see below).

Should you decide to look at bigger companies, they will almost certainly have their own marketing and communications departments. The majority of the work is probably produced in-house but sometimes they need the help of freelance writers, so it doesn't harm to have your name on their records.

Key idea: Lateral thinking

If you want to break into a new area such as writing for business and you have no contacts, it requires a degree of lateral thinking. How can you reach prospective clients? A different route in could be to register your services with the local chamber of commerce or branch of the Forum of Private Business.

Extending this line of enquiry, you can also contact public relations consultancies, corporate publishing consultants and management consultants who all offer communications as part of their services. Again, the majority will be handled by their own staff but, on occasion, outside services are brought in to deal with busy periods.

Make sure you personalize your speculative approach to every company, but bear in mind that this process will be time-consuming as you should only expect a success rate of somewhere in the region of one client for every one hundred approaches. Nonetheless, since the rates of pay are higher in this sector, it can be worth the effort.

WHAT TO CHARGE

Obviously, this is dependent on the size of the company and the nature of the job, but what I would add is that you should not use the rates you get paid for writing for magazines, newspapers or books as a yardstick, as they pay very poorly by comparison to private companies who are used to the rates charged by management consultants and the like. A corporate client will also not blink if you charge travel expenses – although double-check first – so don't be coy in charging what you consider the job is worth.

Some companies are happy to pay an hourly or day rate if it is hard to estimate just how much work is involved – so whatever your normal day rate for magazine or book publishing, you might want to think about doubling it. You can always drop it if they decide to haggle but I suspect they won't, as writers are notorious for undervaluing their specialist skills when compared to photographers, lawyers...

PR agencies are expanding into digital PR and social media and this is creating new vacancies for freelance writers. Agencies have always needed to call on freelance writers at busy times or for specific launches, but now that their clients are handing over responsibility for marketing themselves using social media to outsourced PR companies, there is considerable scope for the IT-savvy writer.

If the more traditional route is your preferred option, then there are still opportunities to be had, especially if you have specialist knowledge, and specialist contacts (either in the business or in the media) to match.

Try it now: Write a flier

It is generally acknowledged that the promotional leaflets and fliers that fall through the letter box have only a few seconds to catch the attention of the homeowner. For that reason, the headline and first sentence have to convey the key message and stimulate interest. It's hard to achieve but not impossible. Practise writing one-page fliers for local events, keeping copy snappy, direct and easy to understand.

Try it now: Write a press release

A press release has to have an eye-catching headline, an engaging story and yet provide all the relevant information, not forgetting contact details in case the media want further information. This is quite an art – why not have a go at writing a press release for a forthcoming event at work or in your community, and see how you get on?

Case study: Sharon O'Connell, Freelance PR Consultant

What does a business client look for in a pitch from a journalist/PR consultant?

'You definitely must be able to show an intelligent understanding and interest of their industry/subject; from a writer's point of view, you should be able to turn your hand to anything and, although there may be some subjects as a writer that you just won't ever feel comfortable with, first impressions are vitally important to securing work, so make sure you do your homework.

'If you are good at what you do, you should be able to summarize anything succinctly, in good English and in a vibrant, usable, grammatical format. There is always the difficulty that, if you put yourself into a niche market, you can lose out on some jobs. So, on the one hand, you could be hired for your specific knowledge, but it is more important to be able to turn your hand to write about anything.'

How do you find clients?

'If you are looking for clients, you have to be as proactive, creative and innovative as possible because it's become a lot harder. So there are several ways. First, let everyone you know in the world know that you are available – everyone does that – but it can't be ignored. So whether that's using networking or personal contacts or going to people you may have just met through other business ventures, network like crazy. Second is to look at specific websites for business writers – one is journalism.co.uk and then go to all the marketing sites as well whether that's Brand Republic, PR Week or Marketing. Also go to the trade press for specialist subjects and look at anything that you think will be able to yield more results or match your style of writing.

'If you find a lead, in PR Week for example, and it's a PR company with a very big corporate client and they just don't have enough people to get the words out, for you to be able to say you have actually had industry experience or you come from this background is useful. But it's that chicken-and-egg scenario – do you get the industry experience first or write something first and try to sell it in? You have to try everything. If you were starting from absolute scratch and you don't have any experience, the best thing is to just write something anyway and give it to somebody else to proof for you and to say whether or not they think that it would be good enough.'

What's the difference between working for a corporate client or for PR doing media relations?

'I think working for a corporate client is less about media relations sometimes. It's very much about long-term image management and the bigger picture. It can be a lot more restrictive; depending on the size of the client, you may come up against other issues such as legalities (what they can or can't say, what they should be seen to be doing or should not be seen to be doing). It becomes a wider remit but at the same time a much more restrictive remit. So, for example, you might have to take into account things like corporate social responsibility (CSR), assisting with professionally written papers, which may not necessarily occur with smaller, privately owned consumer clients. There are some consumer clients who completely leave it in your hands as to how their business should be portrayed in writing and there are others where whatever you write will be sent straight to the legal team.

'The key to good media relations is research – you must understand the publication that you are pitching to. You have to work out the angle for the client: What are they doing that's newsworthy or different? What are they doing that is an improvement on anything already in existence, like new research findings for example? Have they got case studies? What are they doing that will interest people?

'Then you have to translate that angle and tailor it to the publication's style that you're seeking editorial coverage in. So if it's the national press it will be a hard news story; celebrity magazine – has the client treated celebrities? And women's magazines – it's the human story.

'It's also highly beneficial to forge a good working relationship with the journalist/editor. Often, this happens organically when you deliver a good idea or angle and provide the necessary information. Sometimes it comes about when you stay in a specialist area for some time. Yet it still has to be a marriage of the two for sustainability; just because you are on friendly terms, it does not mean the publication will run with your idea.'

Focus points

The main points to remember from this chapter are:

* Writing for corporate clients pays much higher rates than magazine and book publishing.
* There are countless opportunities within business writing not only because of the near-limitless clients but also because of the variety of outlets, e.g. press releases, company histories, management reports, newsletters and employee communications.
* A good way into writing for business is via the trade press or business-to-business publications.
* A specialism can be very helpful in gaining commissions.
* Rather than go directly to corporate clients, you can approach communication service providers such as PR companies, management consultants and corporate communications/publishing companies who sometimes use freelance writers.

Next step

If writing for business is an anathema to you, you might favour the diametrically opposed field of writing for children. Let's move from the corporate-savvy world of PR and marketing to the innocence of children's books in our next chapter. But is it possible to make any money in this genre? Let's see.

11

Writing for children

In this chapter you will learn:

▶ *How writing children's books is much, much harder than people often believe*

▶ *How writing children's non-fiction is generally more lucrative than writing children's fiction*

▶ *The importance of tailoring your language to your age group – in general, your writing needs to be clear and unfussy but never patronizing*

▶ *How creative non-fiction is a growth area in children's publishing.*

Assessment: Evaluate your suitability as a children's writer

Your score from this questionnaire will give you an idea of your suitability for making a career from writing for children:

1 Can you create memorable characters?

      YES   NO   PROBABLY (with practice)

2 Are you connected to your inner child and able to identify with the way a child thinks and feels?

      YES   NO   PROBABLY (with practice)

3 Can you come up with an entertaining storyline that will sustain a whole book?

      YES   NO   PROBABLY (with practice)

4 Can you provide surprises in your story?

      YES   NO   PROBABLY (with practice)

5 Do you have a sense of fun and of the ridiculous?

      YES   NO   PROBABLY (with practice)

6 Do you have a fertile imagination and an enquiring mind?

      YES   NO   PROBABLY (with practice)

7 Can you turn dry factual matter into entertaining events and facts?

      YES   NO   PROBABLY (with practice)

8 Can you come up with original ideas for a well-saturated market?

      YES   NO   PROBABLY (with practice)

9 Can you encapsulate an idea in a couple of sentences for the youngest readers?

      YES   NO   PROBABLY (with practice)

10 Can you still remember your favourite books from childhood?

      YES   NO   PROBABLY (with practice)

There are a few misconceptions surrounding writing for children that need to be dispelled before we get into this chapter. First, just because your children enjoy your made-up bedtime stories, it does not mean that your creations will be a bestselling children's book. And second, the myth that writing a story for small children with half a dozen words on each page must be simpler than writing a full novel is simply not true; in fact, it can be a lot harder.

That said, the children's book market is huge and there is undoubtedly money to be made, albeit not necessarily by being the next J.K. Rowling. Although we'll touch on children's fiction, this market is very competitive. It's hard to crack because no one quite knows why one children's character captures the collective imagination and becomes massively popular while another does not. Who could have known that Postman Pat and his black-and-white cat would succeed where other similar characters had failed.

In fact, the growth market for children's writing is in non-fiction. In 2009 the children's young adult and education non-fiction genre grew by 4.5 per cent in value terms, according to the

Nielsen Book Market Trends report. In part, this is because publishers and authors have in recent years become excited about producing books that inspire and inform children, rather than just lecturing to them. The result is some fantastic non-fiction and a growth market as publishers realize that kids' insatiable curiosity means a bright future for good non-fiction writing.

Remember this: Children tell the truth

Children tell it exactly like it is, so when a child tells you that she loves your book, take it as a genuine compliment.

Children's fiction

If you are still keen to have a go at selling fiction for kids, then there are a few observations to bear in mind if you want to gain the interest of a children's book publisher. Again, as with adult fiction, you are unlikely to attract an advance for your story, so you are effectively writing without payment, and then sending the finished manuscript on spec to prospective publishers. For that reason alone, it is uncommon for novice children's fiction writers to rely solely on this outlet as a way to earn money. In the first instance, it is best to write children's stories in your spare time, while getting an income from other sources. In the happy event that you come up with a marketable idea that a publisher believes can sustain follow-on books, then this is the time to devote all your energies to the genre.

Remember this: Make your book the first in a series

Children are extremely loyal customers and parents are happy to keep buying new books in a series if it means their children are reading. Publishers, of course, know this. So make it clear to potential publishers that your idea is more than a one-off book and that it can sustain a series.

In the meantime, the way to optimize your chances of success with your first book is to give consideration to the following concepts:

▶ **Write for a specific age group** – not only because children's tastes and abilities change, but because publishers market books in specific age bands and it makes it easier for them to envisage where the book sits on their list if its target audience is clearly delineated. (See below for details of age groups.)

▶ **Be original.** It often seems that all the best characters and storylines have already been done to death in children's fiction. Everything from talking trains to magic portals have already been taken, but your idea has to find a new angle on the universally accepted themes of children's books, namely a magical journey, a secret world, being lost, gaining new powers and overcoming unexpected dangers. If you can make your original idea on a trusted theme sustain a whole book, then you may well be on to a winner.

▶ **Be a little bit naughty.** Children are thrilled by rudeness and naughtiness. Anything lavatorial or mildly vulgar that embarrasses adults is guaranteed to delight youngsters. If you don't believe it, check out the number of children's books involving 'underpants' in the heading.

▶ **Create memorable characters.** Lovable or strong main characters together with dastardly villains (think Simba, Mufasa and Scar from Disney's *Lion King*) are essential in good children's fiction. And if they are instantly recognizable as well as memorable, then you have a prime candidate for a merchandizing bonanza – and this is where the real money is to be made. For example, in 2011 *Thomas and Friends* was the number one preschool toy property in the UK for the eleventh year running and the merchandise enjoys similar popularity in Europe and the USA. This follows the success of the TV series *Thomas and Friends* based on Rev. W. Awdry's Thomas the Tank Engine and Friends book series which dates from 1945.

▶ **Take it seriously.** Even if you are writing children's fiction in your spare time, you must still approach the project professionally if you want to get published. So research your topic, if applicable, create your characters and plot carefully, produce a well thought out proposal and show the publisher that you are the right person for the job and that your book has potential and could be the first in a series.

- ▶ **The underdog triumphant.** Given children's status of relative impotence both within the family and the world, certainly in terms of decision-making, it is no surprise that children love stories where the underdog triumphs over the strong. Whether your characters have special powers or are merely able to outsmart their opponents, children find it hugely empowering and appealing to see the weak emerging victorious.

- ▶ **Making sense of the world.** Children are learning all the time about how to operate in the world and how to deal with the problems they might face. If they see a favourite character in a book dealing with dilemmas and making choices, it can help them navigate life's ups and downs for themselves and, without putting too much responsibility on the shoulders of authors, fiction can be a way for them to learn how to empathize with others. That doesn't mean that every book has to be a moral fable, of course, but it can help children to make sense of their world.

Remember this: Heroes and villains

It is fine to have flawed anti-heroes and tragic endings in adult fiction but for children's books the heroes need to win their battles in the end, though the villains can be as cruel, spiteful and sneaky as you like — children love a good baddie.

Children's non-fiction

Non-fiction for children is booming and it's one of the few genres where publishers not only welcome original ideas and proposals but some are even looking for writers to fulfil assignments for them, although, admittedly, the requirement is almost certainly going to be for an agented writer with a proven track record.

While mainstream non-fiction publishers for children are quietly optimistic, those who specialize in books for the school and library markets are especially busy, as changing school curriculums mean openings for new books for children ranging from pre-schoolers and emergent readers to the more complex and in-depth issues covered in books for secondary school students.

And once you are a published author in this market, there is scope to sell features to the growing plethora of children's magazines and websites, which range from simple club titles to glossies and e-zines for every hobby, sport or specialism you can imagine.

Here are a few pointers that can help you to get published and paid in the non-fiction children's book market:

▶ **Narrow down your topic.** Although the range of topics is endless, counter-intuitive though it may seem, don't be afraid to narrow down your subject. For example, instead of writing about the First World War, Michael Morpurgo focused on the microcosm of the role of horses in his best-selling book *War Horse*. Children are interested in details.

▶ **Write age-related books.** Decide which age range you are going to target. There are five categories from which to choose:

▷ *picture books* (0–3 years) where illustrations play as important a role as the text in telling the story

▷ *early reader books*, aka 'easy readers' (5–8 years) aimed at helping a child to expand their vocabulary and reading skills

▷ *chapter books* (7–10 years) with short chapters and short paragraphs for younger readers (these are also available for 9 to 12-year-olds but tackle more sophisticated themes and topics)

▷ *young adult* (12 and upwards) aimed at children who have outgrown chapter books

▷ the fifth subcategory, which is predominantly for boys aged 10–14 years, is intended to *motivate disaffected readers*, as often happens to boys at this age.

Remember this: You don't need to illustrate your book

Unless you (or a friend) are an extremely talented artist, there is no need to supply illustrations to accompany your submission. If a publisher likes your story, they will probably have a freelance illustrator in mind with whom they have worked before. Naturally, you will have some input regarding style but these discussions are held only after your manuscript has been accepted.

▶ **Research the subject.** Publishers prefer to commission a writer who possesses good research skills rather than an expert on the subject who cannot write. So it's icing on the cake if you are a writer with a specialty who can research well, because kids are discerning readers who have an insatiable thirst for new facts. A publisher must be satisfied that you have used reliable sources, interviewed popular experts or celebrities within the field and found as many quirky facts as possible – kids are fascinated by them!

▶ **Tailor your language.** Clearly you have to tailor your vocabulary and style to the target age group but, as a generalization, it should be clear and concise. That said, you can have fun with language – children love onomatopoeia, alliteration, homonyms, double entendres, humour and rhyme. You can build a bond with your young readership by being conversational and talking directly to them by asking questions and using the second person – for example: 'Just imagine if a runaway bull came crashing into your school. You would have to keep cool and act fast.' Irrespective of age group, your passion and enthusiasm for the subject must be conveyed to the reader through the language you choose.

Key idea: Plain and simple

Although it is essential to pitch the language and tone for the age of the reader, that does not mean you have to write childishly. Plain and simple is the order of the day or else it will smack of being patronizing, which kids can spot a mile off.

Finally, once you have produced a successful children's book or series of books, you can extend the earning potential of those titles by getting into talks and festivals. Publishers are keen for authors to promote their books, and local schools, libraries and book festivals are much more proactive now in trying to reach a young audience in whom they are trying to foster a spirit of enquiry and an enthusiasm for reading.

Try it now: Research the market

There is little point in investing time and energy in thoroughly researching and writing your book if there is no market for your topic. Before you start, check out what is currently on the market or on publishers' lists to see if your idea holds water.

Try it now: Creative non-fiction

A genre that is exceptionally popular with children at the moment is creative non-fiction, also known as narrative non-fiction. These are books that read like well-written short stories but are actually factual. If you're not familiar with this style, take a look at the Explorers Wanted series by Simon Chapman. Then why not pick a well-known historical event or character and try to bring it to life in an exciting and accessible way for children.

Case study: Rory Storm, Children's Author

'Publishers of children's books are quite receptive to receiving good ideas and good manuscripts. Once you've got the idea sorted, I find the key to connecting with a young audience is getting the tone and language right for that particular age. A savvy 12-year-old can spot if you are genuinely excited about the subject or if you are faking it. I also avoid using teenage vernacular since, if you get it wrong – and it's very easy to do – youngsters find that cringe-worthy.

'Generally being upbeat and positive is the order of the day. I try to use examples from a child's world to help them to understand complex ideas and information. So, if you are talking about size, then use something familiar to the child as a point of reference, such as "The Nimitz class aircraft carriers are the largest warships in the US Navy. USS *Enterprise* is 1,123 feet long – that's the same length as 14½ tennis courts laid end to end" – a fact I used in an article once.

'In my series of four survival guides, it was a mixture of facts and fictional scenarios (sometimes known as faction) and I brought in lots of devices to involve the reader and keep them engaged. There were questionnaires, quizzes and step-by-step activities, which proved very popular. I found it really uplifting when I got a letter from a young reader with an enclosed photograph of a pot-holder that they had made following the instructions in *The Extreme Survival Guide*.

'A word of caution here, though: if you are going to include activities, you must make sure the instructions are clear enough to follow and are accurate. Let's face it: you are unlikely to get a follow-on title if your publisher receives letters from irate parents saying that a recipe doesn't work or a formula in a science book is wrong. I always used my own sons as guinea pigs to follow the instructions (without interference from me) to make sure the steps were easily comprehensible and that a young reader could produce a finished article, however crude.

'If you hit upon a promising idea for a book, your initial advance for that first book may not be high, but, if it sells well, there's every chance the publisher will then come back to you wanting more books along the same lines, and this is where you can strike a better deal for yourself. As well as *The Extreme Survival Guide*, I also wrote a book for 10 to 14-year-old boys entitled *Castaway Survival Guide*. The publishers were so pleased with the response to these two books that I was commissioned to write a series of four survival guides for the American market – *Jungle Survivor's Guide*, *Sea Survivor's Guide, Mountain Survivor's Guide* and *Desert Survivor's Guide* – which sold very well. So, if your initial idea has legs, it can lead to further, more lucrative commissions.

'Once you are comfortable writing for younger readers, I would advise writers to broaden their horizons. My agent once put me forward to write a kids' non-fiction book on cryptozoology (the study of creatures whose existence has not been substantiated). I certainly wasn't an expert on the subject but, as an experienced researcher, I took on the commission. *Monster Hunt* was great fun to write and proved popular with readers, so I'm glad I took the plunge.

'Children are loyal and enthusiastic fans and they love to meet their favourite authors. Many successful children's writers give talks and tours and speak at festivals and this is another way to increment your income from writing for children.

'There are also magazines and online ezines which require a lot of copy and are always on the lookout for good feature ideas to commission. And you can then turn your specialist knowledge on its head and write for parenting titles with the benefit of the inside knowledge you have gleaned from your young audience. In my experience, diversity is the key if you want to make a living from writing for children.'

Focus points

The main points to remember from this chapter are:

* Non-fiction is a more lucrative market than fiction when writing for children.
* It is a misconception that writing for children is easier than writing for adults; if anything, it's harder.
* You have to target your work for the right age group.
* Don't underestimate the important of honesty or the fun of being rude in children's books, and make sure you do not patronize your young readership or talk down to them.
* To make most money from writing for children, you need a merchandizing package.

Next step

As we have seen, you have to use age-appropriate vocabulary and voice when writing for children. In our next chapter, we look at ghost-writing, where again the voice that you use is not your own – it is that of the book's 'author', which you must capture.

12

Ghost-writing

In this chapter you will learn:

▶ *The broad range of ghost-writing opportunities available – it's not just a matter of celebrity biographies!*

▶ *The importance of setting out clear parameters – fees, deadlines and responsibilities – before beginning work*

▶ *The key skills needed to be a ghost-writer and how to build up trust with your 'subject'*

▶ *How ghost-writers must act as an intermediary between the 'author' and publisher.*

Assessment: Evaluate your suitability as a ghost-writer

How do you think you might fare as a ghost-writer? Fill in this questionnaire to find out:

1 Are you sociable and generally able to get on well with people?

      YES   NO   PROBABLY (with practice)

2 Are you good at putting people at ease?

      YES   NO   PROBABLY (with practice)

3 Are you able to keep secrets and to deal with sensitive issues with complete confidentiality?

      YES   NO   PROBABLY (with practice)

4 Can you cope with 'not getting the credit' for your work?

      YES   NO   PROBABLY (with practice)

5 Can you interpret specialist subjects for the layperson?

      YES   NO   PROBABLY (with practice)

6 Are you diplomatic and patient?

      YES   NO   PROBABLY (with practice)

7 Can you write in a voice that is not your own?

      YES   NO   PROBABLY (with practice)

8 Do your commitments allow you to devote intense periods of time exclusively to being with the subject of the book?

      YES   NO   PROBABLY (with practice)

9 Do you think you will be able to work in close proximity with a celebrity or well-known public figure without being star-struck?

      YES   NO   PROBABLY (with practice)

10 Are you able to identify what is the nub of a story and what is incidental material?

      YES   NO   PROBABLY (with practice)

When you think of ghost-writers, your mind probably turns to books written for big-name celebrities and politicians who do not have the time or the skill to pen their own. You would certainly be right in thinking that ghost-writers are used for these projects, but this genre of writing is much broader than this would suggest.

Many professionals – scientists, doctors, lawyers, financiers and other specialists – want to publish books to establish themselves in their field as experts and to attract clients, but they do not have the time and/or ability to write the manuscript. So, they are willing to pay someone else to put their words and concepts into print.

Alternatively, a publisher may have identified the next big name in a certain field and they want to be the first to publish a book in their name but, knowing that the client is unable to write it themselves, they will find a ghost-writer to work alongside the client.

A less lucrative but possibly more prolific outlet for the ghost-writer is the new and burgeoning family history market. As more and more people become interested in genealogy and tracing their family history or ancestry, so there is a growing interest in committing the findings to print so that the younger generations have this information and it is saved for posterity. With the developments in print and on-demand publishing (see Chapter 9), it is now possible to produce a respectable family history, with or without photographs, at a reasonable price. However, many of those who trace their family history make good researchers but not necessarily good writers, and some are prepared to pay for your professional services as a ghost-writer to tell their story.

The good news is that across the board, there is an increased awareness of the usefulness of ghost-writers, which is driving addition demand. In fact, a report released by freelancer.com shows that, in the United States, the number of outsourced ghost-writing projects climbed by 269 per cent in 2010, and the trend is being echoed in the UK.

 Try it now: Move into family history

If you decide to move into ghosting for the family histories market, you could advertise your services in magazines aimed at an older readership, such as *Saga* or *Yours* magazine, as it is typically the older age group who have the time and inclination to record their lives. Why not buy a copy of such a magazine and see what is already on the market and what it might cost you to advertise, so that you can take this into account when quoting for a job?

Benefits of ghost-writing

For a professional writer who wants to maximize their earnings, the major benefits of ghost-writing are twofold. First, you are being paid to write the book. As soon as it is accepted by the publisher, your job is done and you can move on to the next paying project. So, after typically four to six months working closely alongside the client, you can now walk away and it is up to them to promote their book. This leaves you more time for other writing projects, so increasing your earning potential.

Second, one of the biggest hurdles to earning money from writing is the problem of having to constantly come up with new and marketable ideas. As a ghost-writer, you do not have to come up with brilliant ideas – those are supplied by the client with whom you are collaborating. This takes the pressure off you to constantly find new and fresh ideas and it also saves the time you might spend pitching ideas to publishers without success and, *ipso facto*, without financial return for the effort you have invested in that idea.

Another advantage of ghost-writing, albeit not at first glance financial, is that it's more sociable than writing in solitary isolation. This can make a welcome change for professional writers but it can also result in leads for other work – it's amazing how you hear about things when you're out there and circulating.

Ghost-writing is also a good option for writers who do not have a platform of their own. So, it is the size of the author's platform that will impress (or otherwise) a publisher and your own status does not matter as you are not the one selling and promoting the title.

So, in financial terms, is it worth writing a book for someone else? The simple answer is 'yes'. The majority of people who get publishing deals and require a ghost-writer are able to command a higher advance than you could, and they will probably sell more copies as well. So the percentage you receive as the ghost could well be more than you might earn writing your own book. And if you are being paid a fee by a client (the author), then you can command a good rate, whether you charge by the hour/day, by the word/page, or by the project.

Key idea: Deeper insights

One of the very best things about ghost-writing is the interesting people you gain access to and the inside knowledge you can learn. If your specialist area is the automotive industry and you are paid to ghost-write the book of a mover and shaker in Formula One, for example, you can ask them whatever you like, and gain much deeper insights into your specialism, which you may then be able to use in articles for other publications.

Getting started as a ghost

In addition to the celebrities, experts and everyday people producing memoirs, novels and guides, all of whom want ghost-writers, book publishers, packagers, agents and corporations may also need to hire ghost-writers for specific projects, so there is no shortage of business. But just how do you get your name known?

Remember this: Publish under your own name first

Realistically, it helps if you have published at least one book under your own name before you start ghosting for others, although any writing experience can help you get your foot in the door.

First, you can be proactive and go after ghosting work that might be posted on websites such as craigslist.org, journalismjobs.com, journalism.co.uk and freelancer.co.uk.

At the same time, you need to let people know that you have added ghosting work to your portfolio. So, tell potential clients, editors, agents and publishers in the book trade, and other freelance writers who might pass work your way. You can mention it on your website and blog and add it to your email signature.

You could also consider advertising your ghost-writing services, which can be expensive but if you get one well-paying project after a few months, then it has been money well spent. It can take time for your ad to return a profit, so only advertise if you are able to keep it going for a sustained period. Look at publications such as *The Bookseller* and *Publishing News*.

Try it now: Emphasize your expertise

When marketing yourself to potential clients, emphasize your expertise. I specialize in writing on health and spiritual living, and nearly all of my ghosting projects have been for professionals in those fields. So why not let editors, publishers and colleagues know that you have added ghost-writing to your repertoire?

Making it work

In order for a ghosting project to be profitable, you have to have a good and efficient working relationship with the subject, and that means setting boundaries right from the outset. It is no good agreeing a fee with the client/publisher on the assumption that you will be working from background material, written notes and/or tapes provided by the client, only to find that you are interviewing him or her and writing the book from scratch, which is a far more time-consuming proposition.

These are the sorts of details that need to be ironed out at the beginning of your working relationship and included in the contract. Don't be afraid to discuss:

▶ How the relationship might work – the amount of face-to-face contact and/or email/telephone time

▶ Who is responsible for doing what – the division of labour

▶ Whether you will send the client the book chapter by chapter or as a whole

▶ Who is responsible for expenses incurred

▶ Deadlines – when the background material is due, when the first draft is due, etc.

▶ What you are expected to provide

▶ How much you'll get paid and when (in instalments, on delivery, on publication?)

▶ Cover credit – what's your billing? Are you a co-author and mentioned on the cover, or are you a ghost-writer and only mentioned inside, if at all?

▶ Who owns the copyright – almost invariably copyright is vested in the client

▶ Termination – what happens if either of you wants to back out of the book before it is completed?

Remember this: Share an agent with your 'subject'

When negotiating ghost-writing contracts, it can be very helpful if you and the 'subject' share an agent. In this way, they have both your interests and those of the book at heart, and the publisher is unable to play the two parties against each other over who gets what percentage.

Once you have got all these queries sorted and out of the way, you will then have a clean slate to start working closely with your client. They are effectively investing their trust and their reputation to your skills, so it is important that you do a good job.

Remember this: Make sure you're credited

In general, a co-author is identified on the cover along the lines of 'Celebrity Name with Your Name' or 'as told to Your Name', while a ghost-writer is not named or identified on the cover, although your name may sometimes appear on the flyleaf. However, it's worth asking for a mention or getting a clause in your contract to that effect, since other publishers may notice you, or readers might contact you via the publisher to write a similar story for them.

Ghost-writing skills

The first thing is to make your client feel completely comfortable with you. In the case of a ghost-written 'autobiography', readers do not want the approved, well-honed responses that they see in the media; they want some real insight into the person behind the public image. It's your job to coax the client into answering your questions candidly so that they can reveal more of themselves in your safe hands.

All the same, you must convey the message in the client's own voice. As you spend time with him or her, you will become more aware of manners of speech, character, expressions and views. These are what you have to capture accurately. You have to abandon your own style so that the book authentically sounds as though it were written by the client.

Key idea: Playing second fiddle

Never forget that you are writing someone else's book. Whether or not you are credited, ultimately as a ghost-writer, you must set aside your own ideas if your client disagrees with them, and do it their way. They have the final say.

It helps if you are genuinely interested in the person you are ghosting or in the area in which they operate. It is hard to bring someone's story to life if you yourself are uninterested in what they have to say.

And, if you are keen and interested, then there's every chance that you will foster a close working relationship with the client, which is vital because a successful ghost-writer fulfils many functions. If the client is alarmed by seeing their story warts and all in black and white, it is your job to reassure them that they can change anything they like in the book, even though most will be guided by you as to whether or not it stays in.

Key idea: Indemnification clauses

Make sure your contract includes an indemnification clause so that, as the ghost-writer, you cannot be sued for any libellous or plagiarized material that your client provides. The burden of responsibility rests with them.

It is also up to you to offer reassurance to the client when he or she and the publisher do not see eye to eye over a cover or some publicity for example, since you are their expert in the publishing world. In fact, a ghost often becomes the go-between who smooths the waves that sometimes arise between the client and the publisher. Diplomacy, tact and discretion are needed in spades if you are to navigate the middle ground and to please both sides. The publishers rely heavily on ghost-writers to produce the book on time and without hiccup. They are not really interested in the problems you may have had trying to get hold of the client (those who require a ghost-writer are almost invariably busy people) or dealing with their irrational behaviour. If you want to secure further ghost-writing contracts with that publisher, you have to make the process as smooth as possible and produce the goods without complaint.

Remember this: Be discreet

Most clients will ask a ghost-writer to sign a non-disclosure agreement. Even if they don't, confidentiality is an essential quality in a ghost-writer. If you are indiscreet and tell tales out of school, your ghosting career will be short-lived.

Other outlets

As we discussed, ghost-writers are principally looking at book projects involving either celebrities, captains of industry, public figures, prominent specialists in their field and the personal histories market.

In addition to this, there are some further opportunities for the enterprising ghost. Just as clients may need a ghost because they don't have either the time or skill to write a book themselves, the same holds true for magazine and newspaper articles. Quite often, business leaders, scientists and specialists are keen to write articles to promote themselves or their products or companies in the press, and for this they will need a ghost-writer.

Similarly, celebrities and sports personalities who have guest columns in newspapers and magazines rarely write these themselves. In reality, it is often the job of a staff writer to hammer their views into shape, but if you have access to such people, you could always propose writing material for them on a freelance ghosting basis.

And, lastly, you could adapt your ghost-writing skills to the fiction arena. A successful and long-running series of novels is rarely penned by the same author, especially in the children's market. Publishers will produce as many titles as the market will allow, all following similar lines in terms of style, locations and storylines. If you think you might be able to write a book in a series, whether it is 'boys' own'-style adventures or girls' boarding school romps, while sticking closely to the winning formula, then put together a proposal for the series' publisher.

Try it now: Enhance your social media image

When marketing your specialist talents as a ghost-writer, make sure your social media bios (Twitter, LinkedIn and Facebook) include keywords related to your expertise, whether it's health and fitness, medical or science, or business and finance (not forgetting 'ghost-writer' of course). Also, remember to mention any articles or books you have written in the area, companies you've worked with and projects underway in this niche. And post blogs that mention expertise or tips you might have in this specialty, too.

Case study: Shannon Kyle, Ghost-writer

Shannon Kyle is an author and journalist with over ten years' experience specializing in real-life stories. To date Shannon has written five books, including two Sunday Times *bestsellers,* Forever in My Heart *by Jade Goody (selling over 100,000 copies and spending four weeks at number one on the* Sunday Times *Bestseller List) and* Gypsy Princess *by Violet Cannon (reaching number four in the* Sunday Times *Bestseller List). Upcoming ghost-written titles include* Things Get Better *by Katie Piper,* At the Coal Face *by Catherine Paton Black and* Nobody Cared *by Terrie O'Brian.*

'To be a ghost-writer, you need the same qualities as you need to be a journalist; the ability to listen, to identify the "key stories" in whatever someone is telling you and sometimes the ability to write very quickly. For Jade Goody's book I had just three weeks to do all of the interviews and write the first draft of 75,000 words.

'I've worked as a journalist since leaving university, starting as an editorial assistant at a local newspaper in Staines and working my way up. I've mainly written for women's weekly magazines like *Take a Break*, *Pick Me Up*, *Bella*, *Closer* and *Woman's Own* but was also a feature writer on Sunday tabloid *The People* for a couple of years doing all kinds of writing from editing the Pet columns to doing undercover investigations.

'My big break was when I was offered the chance through a newspaper contact to write Jade Goody's last memoir *Forever in My Heart* for HarperCollins in 2009. I was freelance then.

'You have to leave your ego at the door when you're ghost-writing. It's all about your subject and not you, and the fact you get very little recognition for it when it's published can be a little painful sometimes!

'However, ghost-writing books for others, particularly if the story or person is particularly interesting or high profile, is a real honour and ultimately the books can be bestsellers. When you interview someone about their life story, it also means the plot is already "written" for you and it's a case of capturing their tone and voice.

'My goal is always to make every book sound as similar to the person in real life as possible, so the reader feels as if they're sitting down and being told a story by the subject. One day I would like to publish under my own name, and I have a few plot ideas for novels, but ghost-writing is also very enjoyable and I've learned so much about what makes a page-turning book. Even if nobody knows you have written it, it's very exciting to see your book reach the bestseller list.

'I don't think it's necessary to "like" the person you are writing about, although I've been fortunate enough to work with some amazing and very likeable "authors". At the end of the day, though, I think most people are essentially pleasant and have "likeable" aspects and, even if they do appear difficult or prickly at first, it's likely to be because they are nervous or fearful. Generally speaking, if someone has agreed to do a book, it means they are happy to tell their story and want to get it across as well as possible.

'Although I have been offered ghost-writing projects, I also come up with ideas from scratch on my own. I am constantly finding and looking for good stories and the exciting thing is, you never know what's coming up next!'

www.shannonkyle.co.uk

Focus points

The main points to remember from this chapter are:

* Ghost-writing is an expanding market that is ripe with opportunities.
* It is not only celebrities and sports personalities that require a ghost-writer.
* A successful ghost-writer must suppress their own ego and speak in the voice of the client.
* Ghost-writing books can be more lucrative than writing your own books because you are not involved in time-consuming publicity.
* Building trust and maintaining confidentiality are essential qualities of a successful ghost-writer.

Next step

You have now identified the genres of writing that best suit your abilities and the ones that appeal to you most. Now it is time to look at ways to get your work published and which routes to publication might be best for you.

13

Routes to publication

In this chapter you will learn:

▶ *How to submit your work to the right publisher*

▶ *The advantages and disadvantages of small and big publishers*

▶ *How to find an agent*

▶ *How an agent acts as an important buffer between author and publisher*

▶ *About negotiating contracts and the importance of subsidiary rights.*

In this chapter we are going to concentrate on book publishing. So, before we start, let's get one thing straight – although you may well have heard horror stories about multiple rejections from publishers, the truth is that editors are always looking for new talent, original ideas and good writing; you simply have to give yourself the best chance of getting your manuscript read and accepted.

In 2011 the literary agency Conville & Walsh received 4,800 unsolicited manuscripts. The agency's reader, David Llewelyn, 'sent on' just 144, of which just five received publishing deals. This gives you an idea of the odds. So, whether you are approaching a publishing house directly or trying to find an agent to represent you (both of which have merit), you must optimize your chances by following a few simple guidelines.

Try it now: Back up all your hard work!

What would you do if a house-fire destroyed your home office and your computer along with it? Would your precious manuscript be safely stored elsewhere? If you are not doing so already, get into the habit of backing up computer files and storing them to hand but also in a location elsewhere. Or use an Internet data backup system (such as www.livedrive.com for a small charge per month – currently £4.95) if you prefer – or even both. And *never* send original documents to a publisher or agent without first taking copies – daft though it sounds, people do this!

Finding a publisher

Randomly sending out your manuscript to publishers without researching them first is a sure-fire recipe for rejection. Hundreds of unsolicited manuscripts pass across an editor's desk every month, so if your book does not fit their profile, it will be rejected, possibly without even being read.

The aim when researching the right publisher is to find those whose expertise and track record best fits with your proposal. To find such a publisher, get a copy of a guide such as the

Writers' and Artists' Yearbook or *The Writer's Handbook*
which offer contact details for publishers, plus a brief outline of
their areas of publishing expertise.

Try it now: Make sure your writers' handbooks are up-to-date

If you already have a copy of the *Writers' and Artists' Yearbook* or *The Writer's Handbook*, take it off the shelf and check which year it was published. It comes out annually but people move around within the industry and emphases change, so make sure you buy an up-to-date copy before contacting publishers.

Alternatively, you could go to a bookshop or search online
stores for books already published in your field and check out
the publisher's details. If there are no direct competitors, then
look at books in the same general area – for example, there's
a strong possibility that Godsfield Press, the publisher of Judy
Hall's *The Crystal Bible*, will be looking for other manuscripts
in the mind, body and spirit field.

Once you have narrowed down the list to those publishers who
represent the best option for you – you're aiming for someone
who has books in this general subject area, perhaps written
from a different angle, but not in direct competition with
your own – there is one more consideration: the size of the
publishing house.

Key idea: Standard rejection letters

The vast majority of writers receive a standard no-nonsense rejection letter from publishers that effectively terminates any further interaction. Rarely, a writer receives a rejection letter which invites further dialogue – take this as a signal that your work has plenty of merit and that, with some alterations and reworking, the publisher might be able to collaborate. Sadly, many writers hear nothing from publishers at all – the cruellest of responses but too often par for the course, I'm afraid. Just don't take any rejection personally.

Remember this: Beware the promises of online writing communities

Some online writing communities claim that they will showcase your work so that agents and editors can discover you. Although there are many benefits to being a member of writing groups, online or otherwise, being talent-spotted for a lucrative publishing deal is not one of them. If selling your manuscript is the main pitch of a particular writers' community website, you would do well to be sceptical.

Working with publishers

There are pros and cons for both large and small publishers and, in the long run, it comes down to personal preference and the feeling you get from the individual editors. However, here are a few things to consider.

SMALL PUBLISHERS

▶ Your book may get more attention if the company is producing only a few titles each year.

▶ Smaller teams can often make decisions more rapidly and will make changes more readily.

▶ As a specialist publisher, they know their market inside out.

▶ You are less likely to get a large advance from a small publisher.

▶ Smaller companies may have fewer resources for marketing, publicity and distribution services.

LARGE PUBLISHERS

▶ Large publishers have greater clout with booksellers, so can push for promotions and for stores to take higher numbers of copies.

▶ Advances tend to be higher from bigger companies.

▶ A recognized man can bring prestige to your book.

▶ Decisions take longer to be made and are harder to reverse or change in order to react to an unexpected opportunity.

▶ If you are a small fish in a big pond, your book may not get the promotion or attention it deserves.

Try it now: Choose your best chapters

Included in the standard package that you might send to a prospective publisher or agent is the covering letter, synopsis and three sample chapters. In the case of novels, it would be the first three chapters but for non-fiction it can be the first three or three strong, representative chapters (about 10,000–12,000 words in total). Do you know which chapters you might choose?

Literary agents

If you are writing mainstream non-fiction or fiction, you may be best advised to get an agent, as many publishers now state that they will not accept unsolicited manuscripts.

Having a good agent can be hugely beneficial, although it's not the right option for everyone. We shall look at the pros and cons of having an agent shortly, but first it helps if you understand the role of an agent.

WHAT AGENTS CAN DO FOR YOU

The primary role of an agent is to sell your manuscript and to sell you. They know the market well, which means that they know what publishers are looking for and whom to pitch to. They also know how much a publisher is likely to pay and where there is room for negotiation.

Although giving away 15–20 per cent of all your earnings may seem like quite a lot, having a good agent more than pays for itself. Not only will the agent get you the very best deal possible, they also know contracts inside out, so they are able to barter with seemingly unimportant clauses that can make a big difference to your eventual revenues.

All the time your agent is playing hard-ball with the publishers over your contract, your relationship with the editors remains unsullied. Publishers expect agents to be tough and hard-nosed and, even if you are pushing equally hard behind the scenes, you are not seen to be the unreasonable one. In this way, an agent is an effective buffer between you and your publisher when it comes to thorny issues.

Agents will also invoice on your behalf and chase up monies owed to you – these are tedious jobs that take some considerable time. If you had to do these tasks yourself, you might consider it as unpaid time taken out of your working day when you could be earning.

Finally, once you have developed a relationship with your agent, they can become the best person to advise you on future work. Not only will they have a view on whether or not your next book ideas are viable, they will also be able to put your name forward for projects that they hear about as they go in and out of various publishing houses.

What an agent is not paid to do is to be your editor, nor are they your confidant and friend. This is a *working relationship*. It is in their best interests to get you the best deal possible as they are on a percentage, but listening to you gripe about the unfairness of a writer's lot is not part of the job description.

Here is a summary in brief of the possible pros and cons of having an agent:

Pros

- Some publishers only accept manuscripts that come via an agent.

- Some publishers see an agent as a built-in layer of quality control, since the agent has already rejected manuscripts that stand little chance of finding a publisher.

- Agents know the publishing industry and should not only have good relationships with editors but also know what is trending and what publishers are looking for.

- An agent will do all the negotiation and wrangling on your behalf, leaving your author–editor relationship untarnished.

- Agents sometimes play publishers off against each other, what's known in the trade as a bidding war, so securing you better financial terms.

- ▶ Publishing contracts are complex and intricate and a minefield for the uninitiated. An agent can easily navigate publishing contracts, picking up on questionable clauses and bargaining on various aspects of the deal on your behalf.

- ▶ A good agent should be able to advise you about your proposal and future projects.

- ▶ Occasionally an agent can bring new writing work your way if they hear that a publisher has a book idea and is looking for a suitable author.

Cons

- ▶ Finding a good agent who suits you can be difficult. The best agents are nearly always at or near client capacity, although they are unlikely to turn down a manuscript that is clearly a work of genius or an author who is marketing gold.

- ▶ Some agents do not add value and simply do the job that you could do yourself, while taking 15 per cent of your earnings.

- ▶ If an agent has a bad relationship with a specific editor – it happens occasionally – then it might discourage them from looking at your manuscript.

- ▶ Some editors, particularly in small, specialist non-fiction publishing, prefer to have a direct relationship with the author.

- ▶ An agent is usually looking for the best financial deal for you and could steer you towards the publisher who is paying the most rather than the publisher who best suits you, your book and your future career.

- ▶ If you only want to write one book and no more, an agent may be reluctant to take you on since they are investing time an effort in you with no possibility of future returns.

SECURING AN AGENT

If your favoured publisher will not accept unsolicited proposals, or if you have weighed up the pros and cons and decided to go ahead with finding an agent, where do you start?

The very best way is through personal recommendation, although this connection is not available to everyone, of course. Even if you don't have contacts, you can put out the word that you are looking for an agent and ask whether anyone has any experience they could share with you – you never know what might come up.

You could attend a writing conference in order to meet agents in person, or at least to see them in action. A talk from a leading agent can give you some insight into what they are looking for and what an agent can do for you.

However, even if you recognize an agent that feels the perfect fit for you, it does not mean they will want to meet you for a chat. Telling them that you are a writer and want to find an agent is not enough to lure them from the office. The only thing that will tempt them is a saleable book project. So do not put the cart before the horse – have a finished project to sell before searching for an agent.

Remember this: Trust your instincts

If more than one agent or publisher comes back to you showing interest – a distinct possibility if you have sent multiple submissions – then you must trust your gut instinct over which one to choose, having met them both and satisfied your questions. Chemistry between you and the editor/agent is important as potentially you could be working together for many years to come.

For those who do not have any contacts in the industry, you can look for a suitable agent via the Association of Authors' Agents (AAA) whose members have at least three years' experience and use a standard agreement letter with their authors. There are also lists of agents to be found in the *Writers' and Artists' Yearbook* and *The Writer's Handbook* and on various websites for writers. There are brief descriptions of the subject areas that each agent works in, so only approach those in your particular sphere of writing. Apart from that rather obvious caveat, other considerations such as size of agency, client list, website design or response times are all down to personal taste and instinct.

SIGNING A CONTRACT WITH AN AGENT

The majority of agents now charge 15 to 20 per cent of your advance and of all subsequent earnings from direct sales – domestic and foreign (US sales – 20 per cent) – of your book. You should avoid any agent who wants to charge you to read a manuscript or for editorial services – most reputable agents offer this service for free.

Contracts are usually not too binding. Both sides can sever relations with usually a month to three months' notice. Watch out for contracts that bind you for a set period (a two-year contract, for example) that covers all work produced during that time. If there is anything you either do not understand or with which you are not happy, raise a query about before signing or get the clause removed.

It is generally accepted that any agent who has sold a book to a publisher on your behalf will continue to represent you for that book and take their percentage for so doing, even if you have moved to another agent.

Successful submissions

Eureka – that wonderful moment when your manuscript is accepted by a publisher has arrived. With the elation comes the more plebeian problem of contract negotiation. Of course, if you have an agent, the headache is largely removed, although only you can ultimately decide whether or not you will accept final terms.

If you have gone down the 'un-agented' route and you get acceptance direct from the publisher, you will have to negotiate your own contract. Standard book contracts can be 20 or so pages long and full of inaccessible legal jargon. It is highly advisable to appoint a lawyer specializing in publishing to check the fine details of the contract or to join the Society of Authors to take advantage of their contract vetting service.

The main points will not, of course, be lost on you. All writers can spot the deadline, advance and royalties section of the contract. If you are confident that you can deliver by the deadline, the next pressing issue is how much you will get paid.

According to the ALCS survey, specialist non-fiction authors can expect a typical advance of up to £5,000 while niche literary fiction garners up to £3,000 (maximum advances for mainstream equivalents can be up to ten times as much for ceiling offers). Let us take an imaginary advance of, say, £2,500: a third payable on signature, a third on delivery and acceptance of the manuscript, and a final third payable on publication – pretty standard stuff. The royalties are 7.5 per cent of net receipts. Is this a good deal?

Frankly, it is hard to say. In my experience, publishers are rarely trying to rip you off. There is a little room for manoeuvre but not much, and the figures are not going to move substantially. The only situation where this might not hold true is if you have more than one publisher interested, in which case you can expect the amounts to rise considerably. However, do not get your hopes up, as this is a rare situation.

Nonetheless, a canny writer (and agent) knows that there are areas within a publishing contract where slight increases in the percentage can make a big difference to how much the book earns for you.

Key idea: Free legal advice

The Society of Authors offer free legal advice and a contract-checking service. If you are eligible, it can be worthwhile joining the society to get guidance on draft contracts from either a publisher or agent.

SUBSIDIARY RIGHTS

The way to make your book a more profitable proposition is if you make money from subsidiary rights. Be aware of these clauses in your contract and get the best deal possible in this regard to maximize earnings from your book without any further work.

▶ Serial rights

If the publisher retains serial rights, they will try to sell a serial deal or a one-off extract from the book to newspapers and magazines. Occasionally, they will offer extracts for free just to get valuable publicity for the book.

Serializations are lucrative and you could earn considerably more from a newspaper serialization than from your original advance (the term serialization is misleading – it does not mean a series of extracts but generally a one-off). If the publisher sells a serialization on your behalf, you will be entitled to about 90 per cent of the money (or whatever appears in your contract) but this is set against the advance that has already been paid to you. Even so, it is a good way to help the book to 'earn out' so that you get royalties all the sooner.

Media-savvy agents often seek to retain serial rights when negotiating with a publisher, usually at the price of a slightly lower advance, so they can approach newspapers directly to sell the rights on your behalf. In this way, you get all the money (minus your agent's commission) and it is not offset against the advance.

FOREIGN SALES

A publisher will hope to recoup costs and increase sales by selling the book into foreign markets. Each time a foreign publisher buys translation rights and sells a foreign co-edition, the percentage of revenues agreed comes to you.

If a book has international potential and your chosen publisher is strong in chasing co-editions, then negotiating a favourable rate for foreign sales in your contract can help augment income. Occasionally, an agent will recommend retaining foreign rights if they are confident that they have affiliates abroad who can sell on your behalf. This is a tricky decision for you to make, but, if you have a good relationship with your agent, they should have your (and their) best interests at heart and advise you accordingly.

Quite apart from the additional income, a writer can get a huge buzz from seeing the cover of their book with a foreign title.

AMERICAN RIGHTS

Usually a publisher retains 'English-speaking' world rights, which cover Australasia, South Africa and North America. Occasionally, if your agent has good contacts, then it is worth negotiating the US deal separately (again, you will probably have to make concessions on your advance), but more often the publisher has an affiliate publisher in the US and sales are negotiated internally.

If your book is well promoted in the US, your income will increase exponentially because it is such a huge market.

FILM AND TELEVISION RIGHTS

Should your book catch the attention of a film or television producer, you could hit the payload. Of course, it is rare that a book makes it on to the big or small screen, which is when you start to earn serious money, but it is not unusual for a film or television company to take an 'option' on your book. This means that they buy the rights for the next so many years (as stipulated in the contract) to make a film or programme based on your book. In many cases, the film or programme never gets made during that period, and then they have the option of letting it go, so you can resell to someone else, or renewing it. Some books are optioned repeatedly and the final film or programme never comes out. A great sadness to the writer, undoubtedly, but the small consolation is that it has still been earning him or her additional revenues through the renewed option fees every few years.

SUPERMARKETS AND BOOK CLUBS

Although the percentages earned on sales through these outlets are pitifully low due to the power of the bulk-buying negotiator, they are still sales that you might not normally have received through the normal avenues and, as such, not to be sniffed at. National supermarket chains can shift thousands of copies a day as compared to a couple of hundred through traditional bookshops. Since both supermarkets and book clubs often sell at discount prices, the sliding scale of percentages earned is particularly complicated and best left to your agent when the contract is negotiated.

REPRINTS AND DIFFERENT EDITIONS

If a book is successful, it will be reprinted as a new edition, possibly with a different cover and perhaps with updated material included, for which you will be paid an additional fee. The original version could also be brought out in various guises, for example in a 'large print' edition for the visually impaired. If you have written a series of books for the same publisher, they may combine these in an 'omnibus' edition and republish.

In truth, as a writer, you have very little say in these matters, but when your agent tells you a deal has been struck and you see the bottom-line sales figures heading up, it comes as a very nice surprise.

EBOOK EDITIONS

All traditional publishers now have clauses in their contracts to cover ebooks, but negotiating a good royalty percentage rate for this can increase your revenues from the book. Whereas you might expect 10 per cent of net receipts on hardback and paperback editions, you should be looking for at least 25 per cent for electronic publications.

Despite all these suggestions for negotiation points, before you lose a deal over a minimally increased offer, ask yourself whether you really want to work with this publisher. If the answer is 'yes', then only you can decide whether it is worth jeopardizing a deal by negotiating too hard. Obviously, the advance and royalties are important, but you should also take into account whether this publisher is going to widely promote and market your book and, more importantly, whether anyone else is queuing up to sign you.

Key idea: Good terms

Being comfortable and happy with your chosen agent or publisher can be just as important as getting the most advantageous contract financially. Hopefully, this is going to be a long-term business relationship, so don't sacrifice your first choice for an extra few pounds in your contractual deal.

Case study: Clare Conville, Director of Conville & Walsh Literary Agency

'It depends what state the manuscript is in but if an agent wants to take a writer on, the first thing they will do is look at the existing material or a plan for a proposal. They then, if necessary, should help the author get the material up to the point where it is publishable. I say that because, increasingly, editors do less and less editorial work and so, unless a book is really pretty much there editorially, a publisher will turn it down.

'Leading on from that, having helped the author prepare material for submission, hopefully they will get the author a deal. It might be via an auction in the UK or a number of auctions around the world, or it might be just via someone falling in love with the book and saying they want to publish it. Once the publisher has acquired it, the agent should support the author through the process of editing, copyediting, planning, marketing, publicity, social media, preparation for the publication itself; and at the same time, if the book is right – not all books can sell internationally – selling the book around the world, so ensuring that it gets an opportunity vis-à-vis film rights.

'What excites an agent in terms of a new author varies enormously. It often depends what an agent's passions and interests are. It is often worth checking a company website before submitting. For example I don't do a great deal of romantic fiction or chic lit, so I'm unlikely to fall in love with a book in that genre. Having said that, if someone sends me a modern-day version of *The Pursuit of Love*, I'd go all out to represent that writer. You can check websites, you can look in the *Writers' and Artists' Yearbook*. Also a good tip is to look in the back of the books you love and see whom the author thanks in the acknowledgements; they often thank their agent, so, if you share an interest in the same kind of books, that's another good way of getting a sense of whether an agent you are writing to might like your work.

'I don't think the role of an agent has changed that much with the advent of social media and digital publishing but I think publishing has changed very considerably. In the old days an agent was really a postman. The author delivered the work, then the agent sent it out, did a deal and that was that. Now the agent is very involved in the whole process from the moment the book is sent out and through to publication and beyond.

'As an agent you have many roles; teacher, advisor, financial advisor. You have to multitask as an agent.

'As an agency, we sell all our rights direct, apart from where we have co-agents in the Far East and Eastern Europe, so in that respect we have to be very dynamic, very switched on and very tuned in to what's going on internationally. We work very closely with literary scouts and we sell very widely abroad. I think, in an age where advances are going down in the UK (and I can't see that changing in the next five years given the current gloomy financial forecasts), overseas income can be very important to a writer because in all probability you will not be able to survive on a UK income alone. But not all books sell internationally. If they don't, it doesn't mean it's not a good book; it just means it can't travel in the marketplace.

'I always say to all of my authors, "Please, don't give up your day job," unless I can see that the income is going to be really significant. It's really hard to earn a living from writing. That's not to say you shouldn't aim to do it. Certain writers set out to extract huge sums of money from the marketplace and sometimes they succeed, but I think that it's ill-advised to assume that, as a writer, once you've sold your novel it will be a pot of roses. Most books fail in the marketplace. You have got to write for a lot of reasons. One – because you really love it; and two – because, if you like, you have to want to share a story with as broad a readership as possible. Of course, it's great if you can make money out of it and an agent's job is to maximize that potential for you. But If someone came to me and said that, "I just want to make a lot of money out of this," I'd probably tell them that they'd got the wrong agent.

'I think longevity now is really about classic status. Books as diverse as *The Valley of the Dolls*, *The Group* or *Decline and Fall* can be re-promoted and resold and have achieved classic status, but most backlist is eroding. In the old days, there was much more author loyalty from readers. Nowadays, a writer picked up by Richard and Judy can sell 100,000 to 150,000 copies of their book and everyone thinks that's it – that's great – and then their next book sells 5,000 copies because there is no loyalty to the originating writers. The interest is in the taste of the club.

'So can an agent help prolong an author's career? Up to a point. The market factors, quality of writing, the changing faces of digital, fashion, age – all these play their part and an agent can have a degree of control but not total control over it.'

Focus points

The main points to remember from this chapter are:

* If you are given the option, you have to decide whether it is best for your book to be a big fish in a small publisher's pond or to enjoy the clout of a big publishing firm, where you are one among many authors.

* If you only want to write one book, it may not pay you to get an agent but some publishers will only consider submissions through agents.

* An agent is qualified to get you the best deal possible and is a buffer between you and the publisher, especially when it comes to difficult negotiations.

* Publishing contracts are extremely complex and yours should be checked by a qualified person, namely your agent, a writers' association such as the Society of Authors or a media lawyer.

* Understanding and getting the best percentages on subsidiary clauses can positively affect your potential earnings from a publishing contract.

Next step

Irrespective of whether you are publishing a book, writing for the print or broadcast media, or taking on ghosting and business writing projects, the important thing is that you know how to market and sell both yourself and your work. And we'll find out how in the following chapter.

14

Marketing and promotion

In this chapter you will learn:

- *How to market your writing across a broad range of media*
- *How a human-interest story can be an important hook on which to hang your work*
- *How to use your specialism to reach as many markets as possible*
- *How to develop a significant 'web-presence'.*

Sad to say, there are countless talented writers who give up or who spend their career earning a pittance, not because they are without talent, but because they don't know how to market themselves and their products effectively. Realistically, as a freelance writer, you have to remain motivated and professionally determined if you are to succeed – and, as a one-man marketing band, you must take every opportunity to show yourself in the best light and to as many useful people as possible, because no one else is going to bolster your career for you.

It is clear that all writers face rejection and knock-backs during their career but you must not let such negative feedback affect your ability to sell yourself and your work with confidence. Professional writers need to keep faith in their abilities at all times and keep selling their ideas, products, services and professional persona.

Try it now: Plan a launch

The publication day of your book is a very big deal for you but it is all in a day's work for your publisher and agent, so unless you have organized it yourself, don't expect a book launch or fanfare. It is still a good reason for celebration, so why not plan your launch and draw up an imaginary invitation list.

Whether you are talking to editors about regular work in their magazines or helping your publisher to promote your book, basically the majority of the energy and enthusiasm for the project will come from you. In the case of a book launch, you can count on the support of your publisher's publicity department for about a month before and after the launch, and that is it. So the best person to rely upon is yourself.

Naturally, you should cooperate with the publicity team as much as possible and be as supportive and enthusiastic as you can for as long as you have their full attention; after all, they may well be able to get you media interviews and generate column inches in the print media that you are unable to get yourself. However, the best investment of your time is in coming up with promotion angles and leads that they may not have thought about.

Angles

Whether you are publishing a non-fiction mainstream or specialist book, or a novel, no matter how good, its launch among a sea of other titles is not that newsworthy and, as such, is unlikely to attract media interest. However, if the author or the content has a good human interest story attached to it, then this might be something that would interest a journalist or editor. Look for the personal story angle and put it to the publicity department to work on.

When I wrote a self-help book about the 'sandwich generation' entitled *You and Your Ageing Parents: How to Balance Your Needs and Theirs* based on my own experiences of looking after ageing parents while trying to raise a young family, the personal story captured the eye of journalists and I was interviewed for women's magazines and newspapers. As is the way with the media, once it was picked up by one publication, others followed the story up. I was then interviewed by the *Guardian* and other national newspapers as well as by national radio and that led to numerous regional and independent radio stations wanting me to talk about the book. The book even made it onto Google Alerts. The best spin-off – and I have to say, this outcome is rare – is that I then got invited to do the ITN live newspaper review, billed as the author of 'a wonderful new book'.

PRINT MEDIA

As you can see, if the human-interest story strikes a chord with journalists, it only takes one to start the ball rolling – although, be warned, if your story is published in one title, no competing titles will then give you coverage. There is a distinct pecking order to this publicity exclusivity competition:

a national newspaper will not profile you or your book if it has appeared in another national. Women's magazines see themselves as distinct from newspapers but they have their own priority system, so, again, coverage in one precludes a piece in another. However, a major regional newspaper will not mind if a national or a magazine has run a piece on you, and a small regional newspaper has no qualms about exclusivity at all.

A review of your book – assuming it is positive – in a newspaper or magazine is quite a coup in terms of publicity. You needn't worry about bad or vicious reviews as these are very rare, as editors usually prefer to devote column inches to the many good books on the market.

Key idea: Engineer a link

Most major mainstream newspapers have specialist supplements such as health, travel, science and technology, finance and so forth, especially in their weekend editions. If your new book has any connection with the subject matter, however remote, it is worth engineering a link and getting publicity to send a press release.

SPECIALIST JOURNALS

And don't rule out specialist journals. The link may be tenuous but, if your novel is set in the property market, *Professional Surveyor Magazine* may jump at the chance to publish a book review – as it makes a welcome relief from turgid tomes on surveying. It might not have an enormous readership but it is targeted and less of a scatter-gun approach than a review in the mass-market publications.

The bottom line is that you must furnish your publicist with as much information as possible, whether or not you think it is relevant to the book. Mention that you competed for England's youth basketball team or that you have adopted Zambian children or that you nursed your husband through a debilitating illness or that your father was a signatory at the Handover Treaty signing in Hong Kong – all right the last one is improbable but you get my gist. Give the publicity department the fullest possible picture of you and angles for the book and let them decide what is relevant and what is not.

Remember this: Nothing ventured...

Ask to see the list of publications, radio and television programmes and other media that your publicist plans to approach. If you have others to suggest, add them to the list. If the publicity department are reluctant to follow up your suggestions, then contact them directly. Nothing ventured, nothing gained.

RADIO AND TELEVISION

Independent and local radio stations have countless hours to fill with next-to no budget, so they represent a good opportunity for publicity, usually in the form of an interview or appearance on a phone-in chat show.

Television is a much harder nut to crack but, as we've seen, if you have a strong human-interest story or it is something that is in tune with a topical news story, then an invite might be forthcoming.

I was invited on to BBC One's *The One Show* as the author of a book called *Revenge* to fit in with a feature they were covering. On the day of my appearance, our slot was dropped at the last minute because the story was knocked out of the news by the bust-up of a super band, and the producers decided to run a story on sibling rivalry instead – another useful lesson in the vagaries and pitfalls of the publicity circuit.

Remember this: Printed versus broadcast publicity

Although radio and television appearances have a high impact and are highly desirable owing to high listening and viewing audience figures, remember that publicity in print has a longer shelf-life, and people can refer back to printed publicity if they forget your name or the name of the book – something they cannot do with broadcast publicity.

INTERNET

The jury is still out on the benefits of using websites and forums of social media such as blogging, YouTube, Pinterest, Facebook, Twitter, LinkedIn and so on as a way of self-promoting and publicizing your book or writing. Nonetheless, until there is a definitive answer, it seems mad to pass up any opportunity that might add to sales.

Of course, if you have a booming website with a healthy fan base or you regularly tweet to thousands of followers, then it makes sense to keep plugging your own book.

Without that platform, it is harder to get your publicity plug noticed among the sea of 550 billion online documents. The key is getting other sites and other bloggers to link to you and to get your tweets re-tweeted. If you can find an unique angle or something genuinely humorous, then there is a chance that your offering will strike a chord and it could go viral – but do not count on it. This is a rare occurrence and no one has the formula for what will capture the imagination of those in the ethersphere.

Similarly, even if you do manage to sell some copies of your book through links with other sites, it is not likely to be in significant enough numbers to have any real effect on your income. However, full-time writers and journalists are pretty much agreed that blogging, tweeting and online posting are essential tools in the professional writer's armoury. More importantly, your publisher's publicity department may now expect it of you.

In fact, Internet giant Amazon are so sure that social media is the way ahead for self-promotion for authors that their audio arm, audible.com, announced in April 2012 that they are making a $20 million (£12.5 million) fund available to authors who go out and find their own readers. Authors who sign up will be encouraged to use social media to promote their work, and will receive $1 for every audiobook sold from audible.com, audible.co.uk or iTunes, on top of their royalties.

Become an expert

As an author, your other angle could be that you present yourself as an authority on the subject of the book. Of course, if it is a specialist title rather than a broad-spectrum book, this is somewhat easier but the principles remain the same. As an expert, you will probably have useful connections within the field, and publishers will want to make as much use of those as possible. For example, if your book relates to restoring a vintage Alvis motorcar, then you will almost certainly be in touch with the Alvis Owners' Club and other classic car members' clubs and associations, all of whom possess targeted mailing lists and probably websites with online communities. It is not hard to see how these contacts might be very useful in marketing your book.

Try it now: Use a light touch

If you are directly targeting a specialist mailing list for marketing purposes, make your approach gentle and helpful, humorous even. You do not want to annoy the recipients, who after all are not expecting to hear from you, so use a light touch.

FEATURES

Why not look in to whether there are major festivals, or in the case of the above illustration, vintage car rallies, where you could promote yourself and your book. It's unlikely that any actual sales will cover the costs of travel and accommodation (which will hopefully be picked up by the publisher), but, as a loss leader, it is spreading the word and helping to establish you as an authority in a specialized world.

Another string to your publicity bow is if you can write features to support the book (if you have written the book, presumably this should not pose too much of a problem to you). For a professional freelance writer, this can be galling because it is unlikely that you will get paid. Nonetheless, several well-placed articles that make reference to your book and reach an audience that you might not otherwise have had access to could be worth the investment of your time.

Try it now: Make a list of feature ideas

Over the next few days – this is not something that can be dashed off – come up with a list of feature ideas that you could write and ideally publication slots into which to place them, as a way of broadening your publicity campaign.

Direct sales

There is a good chance that you will be able to buy copies of your book at a heavily discounted rate, and as long as there is no stipulation in your contract to say otherwise, you can sell these copies into other outlets yourself at whatever price you choose.

If you sell it to other outlets, you will not be making a direct profit as you will have to sell at wholesale prices, but you will be getting the book noticed by a broader audience and, ultimately, your efforts may well be reflected when the next royalty statement arrives.

Key idea: Buy up your out-of-print books

If your publisher allows your book to go out of print, they will usually allow you to buy up the remaining copies at a ridiculously low price – we're talking pence – rather than pulping them or selling them to a remainders shop. If you have a platform such as a website or you run workshops, you can then sell these copies direct to the public.

Case study: Harry Bingham, author of *Writers' & Artists' Yearbook Guide to Getting Published* and founder of The Writers' Workshop

'There's a lot you can do to help your publisher to market and promote your book, but each campaign needs to be shaped to suit around you, your book and your existing connections and assets.

'I was asked to write *Getting Published* because, as boss of The Writers' Workshop, I already had plenty of assets when it came to marketing writing-related ventures. So I worked these to the full when I had a book to promote.

'You should not expect a publisher to spend very much money on marketing your book. Few non-fiction titles will repay any real outlays of cash, so you need to adjust your expectations accordingly. But that doesn't mean a publisher should be idle. They need to be thinking of:

► How to maximize their own web-presence in the area

► Any stories they can generate in the national press

► Useful approaches they can make in the regional or specialist press

- Ways they can work with specialist websites or membership groups in the appropriate field (e.g. if your book is about historic houses, they might be looking to partner with the National Trust in some way)

- Pitching you as a speaker at festivals

- Creating competitions (typically on launch) which might get the word out through the social media

- Using their own mailing lists and social media tools

- Getting review copies of your book out to appropriate bloggers

- Co-branding the book with other sister publications.

'None of these things costs the publisher any money directly – it's much more about time and effort – but you do have a right to expect that kind of effort.

'A book that has no sales support will not sell, whereas an energetically supported book has a good chance of becoming the dominant title in its niche. But also, from your point of view, you quite likely have a portfolio of interests. So, in my case, I'm not just the author of *Getting Published*, I also make money from speaking fees, from driving interested readers to The Writers' Workshop website, and so on. If you find ways to make money across a range of linked activities, you'll find the returns to each marketing endeavour start to look quite strong.

'You probably won't get a review in newspapers – the review pages have much less space than they used to and they now represent only a relatively narrow range of titles. Specialist magazines are much more hopeful. (So your *Practical Fishkeeping* should be a dead cert as a review possibility for *The Fishkeeper's Monthly*.) Amazon also matters a lot. The more reviews you can solicit, the better. People don't just look for the average number of stars, but for the total number of reviews. A book that has been reviewed 30 times seems much more authoritative than one that has been reviewed just once or twice. And those Amazon reviews are for ever, so a well-reviewed publication will sell and sell and sell.

'The benefit of using social media depends very much on you and your profile. Merely having a blog or a Twitter account is meaningless. What matters is the degree to which you have a large and engaged audience. You won't get that audience simply by publishing a book – aside from your mum, no one really cares. So really the question is: Will your existing portfolio of activities support a busy digital presence? If the answer to that question is 'yes', you should certainly be doing what you can to support and maximize that presence.

'The whole process of building a substantial Web-presence is too big to go into here, but do be aware that purely static websites (that is, ones that aren't constantly updated via new blog posts) are of limited use these days. It's also worth remembering that things such as Twitter are not a form of broadcast media (where you simply announce stuff to the world), they're a form of social media (where you engage with the world). If you don't engage, you won't get any significant traffic.'

Focus points

The main points to remember from this chapter are:

* Despite the inevitable rejections, always sell yourself and your work with confidence.
* Cooperate fully with the publicity team but also be proactive in coming up with publicity ideas.
* Look for the human story either in the book or your own life to help attract the attention of the media.
* Sell your knowledge as an expert and get publicity in that way.
* Always look for interesting angles for publicity and broaden your media net by looking at specialist journals as well as mainstream media.

Next step

You have now ticked all the boxes, and only you can decide whether or not you are cut out for a life as a freelance writer. But before you make up your mind, take a look at the final chapter where we discuss some of the aspects of the lifestyle you may not have considered.

15

The art of freelance living

In this chapter you will learn:

- ▶ *How to manage your finances and keep on top of your accounts*
- ▶ *The importance of having a good accountant*
- ▶ *How to flourish as a freelancer and to weather the ups and downs*
- ▶ *How to keep inspired.*

You should by now have decided which genre of writing best suits your abilities, whether you can cross-promote and work in several areas, and whether you're cut out for a life as a full-time freelance writer or prefer to dabble your toes in the freelance pool while still gainfully employed elsewhere.

One of the key things to keep in mind is that you are not going to be an overnight success as a freelance writer, whichever genre you choose. A freelance career is a slow-burner and, in the beginning, commissions and income are going to be in short supply – but it does get better. Sadly, many writers give up because the initial tough stage lasts longer than they had envisaged. In fact, the rewards of regular work and the occasional perk may come thick and fast once you have ridden out the early dearth of opportunities, dispiriting though this starting-out period may be.

The battle cry of the freelance writer is: 'Never, never give up.' Keep plugging away, adapting your approach, coming up with new ideas, exploring new subjects and, if you are repeatedly knocked back, then finding other angles and other outlets to try.

As long as you keep the above criteria in mind and you always keep the needs of both your target audience and the commissioning publication in mind, then you will eventually start to get results. Commissioning editors, agents and publishers are like anyone else – if someone makes their job easier by providing them with solutions rather than more questions, they will jump at the chance.

Even if you have passed the difficult early years and you are now an established freelancer, it is important to stay inspired and to keep intact that healthy curiosity, a nose for a good story and the love of writing that got you into the profession in the first place. So don't sequester yourself away in your office – get out in the world where the real action is and get inspired.

And, most importantly, despite the inevitable rejections that all freelance writers receive, you must continue to believe in yourself, your abilities and your writing. Only if you are armed with this self-belief and a strong professional determination will you be able to continually market yourself effectively. At the end of the day, it is this one-main marketing campaign that will get you the work.

Freelance finances

We have talked about the importance of perseverance, of staying inspired and of marketing yourself. The final cheese in the freelance Trivial Pursuits game is to master the finances of being a self-employed writer. Like all small businesses, neglecting this area of your operation could scupper your plans to live the unfettered life of a freelance writer.

As a full-time freelance writer, all of your income from writing – be it from journalism, book publishing or speaking engagements – is taxable. However, the good news is that you can offset plenty of expenses for tax purposes. So research materials (books and magazines), travel and subsistence, office equipment, stationery, phone bills and so on are all valid expenses. Writers are notoriously bad at claiming what they are entitled to because, much of the time, they do not feel that the non-writing things they do constitute as work. However, if you get inspiration for writing an article while wandering around the Viking ship at Sutton Hoo, then your entry ticket and travel expenses are reclaimable. If you are invited to lunch with your new agent, the same holds true. It may feel wrong because these are pleasurable pursuits, but these are legitimate claims – it's one of the perks of being a freelancer.

Remember this: Getting a mortgage as a freelancer

Although genuine expenses set against earnings often mean that you pay very little to the taxman. It also means that on paper you are earning peanuts, which is not so useful if you want to get onto the property ladder. If you do not have a second income through another job or a high-earning partner, this could be problematic if you want to get a mortgage.

In a similar vein, if you work from a home office (and no freelance writer at the start of their career should consider paying for an office), even if it's a corner in a shared room, the costs are allowable for tax purposes. Clearly, you cannot put through all your household bills when you are only using one room, but you can put a percentage of the total running costs – rates, rents/mortgage, electricity, gas, water, insurance and so on – through as a taxable expense.

Try it now: Look out for good deals on home office equipment

You have a lot of capital outlay when you first start out as a freelancer. Admittedly, you can get equipment such as office chair, desk and separate telephone line, IT items such as computer, printer and digital voice recorder and stationery (headed or otherwise) as and when it is required, but this is all necessary and eventually unavoidable expense, so why not start checking out the online and discount stores for the best deals.

Your accountant – and yes, unless you are exceptionally good with numbers and tax returns, an ordinary high-street accountant is advisable – will be able to calculate what percentage to charge based on the number of rooms (excluding kitchen and bathroom) you have in your house. They can also advise on schemes run by the Inland Revenue that help writers who may have an erratic income to average their annual incomes if it is of benefit.

Try it now: Planning to work for a US outlet? – Get an ITIN

If you plan to write a blockbuster screenplay for Hollywood, or a more modest feature for an American magazine, either way you will need to obtain an Individual Tax Identification Number (ITIN) from the IRS in order to make a sale into the US. You will have to jump through hoops to get it, so it could be worth checking out the website now (see 'Further sources of information') but it is worth it if you plan to work regularly for American media as it will help to minimize your taxation.

Sometimes, out of the blue, an unexpected payment comes along. Perhaps your publisher sells a co-edition of your book to Spain and you get a cheque for £1,000, or a feature that you sold to a women's magazine is accepted by a specialist title, so, with the minimum of work, you have earned an additional couple of hundred pounds. No matter how successful, these unexpected windfalls are welcome but when you are most in need of them, at the beginning of your career, sadly they are usually fewer and further between.

STAYING AFLOAT

Only you can know what you need to earn from writing in the first few years in order to survive. Clearly, some months will be better than others but there is a bottom line that you have to achieve across the year, which helps you to decide what you charge and what you can afford to accept or not.

This is in the ideal world, of course, but in reality freelancers tend to accept whatever is offered in the early years. If you are not working one day and you are offered a job, even if it is below your hoped-for rate, you accept it because it is better than earning nothing.

Similarly, if you are offered a feature commission at £100 per thousand words, that is not a good rate but it is far from rare. Perhaps if you know you have access to all the research already so it won't be an arduous job and you can probably complete it in a day, rather than the usual two or more, then it is worthwhile, even if you could get paid twice that much elsewhere. It's a bird-in-the-hand, as they say.

Unfortunately, no one can afford at the beginning to turn away work. That is a luxury that comes later in your career when there are more better-paid options available to you. Initially, you take any paying job that gets you an established track record, and you keep your eyes open for the occasional story that earns you more money. Once you are established, your rates go up and you can pick and choose your jobs a little more.

Key idea: Keep on top of your payments

The biggest enemy of the freelance writer is cash flow. You cannot count on any deal until the contract is signed and publishers (magazines in particularly) are notoriously bad at paying on time. So keep a close eye on what is owed to you, start chasing in good time, send a statement as a reminder (some companies will not pay until a statement is received), and never count on money being in your account on time.

Whether you are working by day rate or commissioned word count, freelance writers rarely get paid instantly for their work. Usually, you have to invoice when you submit the feature and then payment is on publication or a set number of days thereafter. In the case of a monthly magazine, that means you may have to wait as much as four months for payment. With newspapers, the lead-in times are shorter so payments are made more promptly but, still, your invoice won't be paid until after your feature has appeared in print. Nonetheless, it is helpful to know that magazines, newspapers and book publishers all have their own set procedures regarding payment terms; if you know what these terms are, then you can predict when monies will be coming in, which in turn can help with cash flow. However, you still have to stay on top of things and chase payments as soon as they become due.

Finally, almost every freelance writer has at some point in their career been faced with a bad debt – either a company that refuses to pay or has become insolvent owing you money. Apart from trying to avoid commissions from any company that you suspect may be financially instable, there is not much you, as an individual with no leverage, can do.

It helps if you have a larger organization behind you. So, if you're a journalist, membership of the National Union of Journalists, for example, can offer you some protection as, in certain cases, they will chase overdue payments for you. If you are not a member of a professional body, you could pursue a claim through the small claims court but, if you are expending a lot of time and nervous energy on chasing this one payment, this is eating into your available time to earn more money. It is clearly a judgement call that only you can make, but you may be best advised to let it go, putting it down to experience, and to try to recoup your losses by selling the article (or a reworked version of it) to another publication.

Try it now: Don't threaten – explain your situation

In my experience, when payments are long overdue and you really need the money you are owed, threats have very little effect. Being honest and explaining that you are getting desperate usually elicits a more sympathetic and positive response. However, be aware that the hands of the accounts department are often tied as all invoices have to be signed off by the powers-that-be; and they tend to remain unmoved by your pleas.

The freelance lifestyle

At the beginning of your career, you should give it very serious consideration before giving up the day job. Although writing for money (freelancing) is not always easy if you are also trying to maintain a full-time job, the safety net of regular payslips may be essential. Initially, you may only earn 'pin money' from your writing but eventually you may get enough commissions for your salary to simply stop the occasional gaps in your freelance earnings. At that point, you might like to give up the other job, but probably not before.

In the meantime, if you are finding it difficult to juggle both commitments, perhaps your full-time employer might entertain the idea of you cutting your hours. Maybe you could find a different job that is less stressful and full-on, which pays the bills but does not overburden you, and allows you to write more freely.

Once you have reached the happy position of being a full-time writer, then you have to maintain your status as a freelancer. Sometimes that means being versatile and not only accepting but seeking out jobs in different spheres than your normal writing activity. Believe me, you will thank me later if you take this one piece of advice to heart.

When you are starting out, it's a temptation to say 'yes' to everything however unreasonable the deadline or request. And that's as it should be. But if you suspect an editor is exploiting your eagerness, perhaps expecting you to write for just a by-line, then do not be afraid to say 'no'. There will be other opportunities and occasionally an editor will reconsider once they realize you are not a desperate doormat. Trust your instincts and you will not go far wrong.

There is one final piece of gritty realism before we finish. Artistic integrity has no place in the vocabulary of the freelance writer. That is not to say that you should not have integrity about your writing, but if you are repeatedly told in rejection letters that your book is too long and needs editing down, and this is a view echoed by your agent, then you would be daft not to sacrifice your artistic integrity by losing several thousand words.

Remember this: Reinvest

Once you start to earn over and above your essential needs, it is worth reinvesting those funds into your business. If you bought the cheapest start-up equipment, then upgrade your computer, laptop or printer. Consider investing in a better website or advertising campaign to raise your image.

STAYING INSPIRED

If you still enjoy the writing process, you remain curious and inquisitive, and you are still marvelling at the fact that someone wants to pay you to do what you love, then being a freelance writer is the right job for you.

Clearly, there are obstacles to staying the course. Even after your first flurry of commissions, contacts move on, publications fold, policies are changed – it's a sad reality. Nevertheless, if you take sensible precautions – such as not relying on a sole publication or media organization for all your revenue – and recognize that setbacks are a fact of life in the freelance world, you are better equipped to face the usual ups and downs of a normal writing career. It is rarely plain sailing, but the unexpected is not always a negative – sometimes it's an unexpected jolly that leads to a lucrative job. The uncertainty is one of the perverse charms of the job.

And, although it is tough at the start, a hard-working writer should end up earning substantially more as their career progresses. As long as you are able to write efficiently, manage your time and finances well, and market yourself and your product successfully, then you are in very good shape to survive the vagaries of a freelance lifestyle.

Remember this: Keep sending out proposals

Ideally, you need to be sending out ideas and proposals for the next commission before the current job is finished, or else the work will dry up. In reality, you are so busy meeting deadlines that there is little time to scout for new work. These time constraints lead to peaks and troughs in workload, so try to spend an hour or so a week to concentrate on future projects and to sound out prospective commissioners.

Writing for a living is one of the most satisfying ways to spend your time and there are enough commercial opportunities to keep the diligent and resourceful freelance writer occupied. Whether you decide to focus on one of the many genres of writing covered here or to experiment with a portfolio of different outlets that you had not previously considered, I hope you enjoy your writing.

You may decide that you want to keep your freelance writing as a welcome additional income while you continue in your day job. Conversely, it may be a lifelong ambition to earn a living as a writer, and nothing less will satisfy.

Whatever your choice, I hope you enjoy the writing, the excitement, the satisfaction and the variety that comes with a career in freelance writing.

Case study: Charmian Evans, freelance writer for print and broadcast media

'I've been a journalist since the mid-70s – magazine, newspaper, radio and some TV work. I've worked as a staffer, a retained journalist and latterly as a freelance journalist. I moved down to Plymouth from London and have taken my retained jobs with me but have gone freelance to give myself more scope to work for a variety of newspapers and magazines without being tied.

'The thing to bear in mind if you move away from London is that the amount of freelance that you can do for local magazines and newspapers is minimal and it's very poorly paid. Even the nationals are not paying as well: years ago I can remember doing a feature on Damon Hill and getting paid £5,000 for 1,000 words. Now I would probably do the same piece and get maybe £500.

'So things have changed an awful lot with the economy. It's much harder getting things placed now simply because there is a stratum of editors that has been cut out of most newspapers and magazines and they are all multitasking. A lot of magazines and newspapers are not commissioning very much now.

'After all that, if you are a creative bod, there is absolutely nothing more satisfying than writing a feature and honing it and crafting it. It's just the most energizing, exciting and great feeling, and I love it. And I'll do it until the day I die because the one good thing about being a journalist is that, if you're a good writer, your writing actually improves as you get older, I believe. You have more confidence to put down what you want, you believe in things more passionately and therefore you can write about it better, and you just have more life experience.

'I think that for me journalism has been a fabulous job. I've travelled all over the world and met all sorts of people and done all sorts of things I never would have done had I gone into something different.

'Regarding freelancing, I think the key to success is that you have to multitask. If you only want to write about beauty, then the outlook for you is maybe not so optimistic. I have many a time had the phone ring and got a commission from an editor and my mouth has said "Yes", and my brain has said "No" and I've almost wanted to go into the foetal position under the desk, thinking "How on earth am I going to write a piece about the economic climate of Cornwall?" or something equally out of my comfort zone. But you do it because it's a challenge. I've really written on everything from pins to elephants over the years and I think that's what is exciting about it.

'So you've got to go into freelancing really being open, and the other thing that is so important is that you've got to have a good news nose and to really keep your eyes open for opportunities all around you, whatever they are. It could be that you're a mum at home and your child is sitting A levels and it's really stressful. Instead of just thinking about it, if you've got a journalistic head on your shoulders, you'll turn it into a story that has empathy with all the other mums – and dads, of course – who are going through exactly the same pressures of moody, stressed youngsters who make a moody, stressed family.

'We all get writer's block occasionally, but more so as a freelancer because you don't have the pressures of the office around you to galvanize you. My cure for writer's block if I get it, and it's rare these days, I write an email to a friend. Just a warm, flowing email and it oils my writing thoughts and I can come back and start writing straight away without any problem.

'Staying fresh and motivated as a freelancer comes with your personality and it's something that you can't learn. You have to be pushy, you have to be excited about life. You have to be disciplined. And you have to have a good news nose – to see things that come up and think, "That's a good story, I'd like to do that." You have to be curious. These things you can't learn at university and you can't read in a book. I always reckoned when I used to interview people for jobs, you could spot the people who were going to make it a mile off and, if you're not motivated like that, you haven't got a hope.'

Focus points

The main points to remember from this chapter are:

* Don't give up the day job straight away as it is difficult to earn a living initially from writing alone.
* Persevere and stay positive as it can take up to ten years to establish yourself as a freelance writer.
* Do not neglect your accounts – you have to run your freelance career like a small business.
* Be as versatile as possible and explore various genres of writing – this keeps a steady flow of income.
* If you remain curious and interested and still love to write, a career as a freelance writer is hard to beat.

Further sources of information

Books

Eats, Shoots and Leaves by Lynn Truss (Fourth Estate)

Fowler's Modern English Usage, re-revised 3rd edn by R.W. Burchfield (Oxford University Press)

Writers' and Artists' Yearbook (A&C Black)

The Writer's Handbook (Palgrave Macmillan)

The Guardian Media Directory (Atlantic Books)

Benn's UK Media Directory

Willings Press Guide (Hollis Directories)

Writers' & Artists' Yearbook Guide to Getting Published by Harry Bingham (A&C Black)

Write Fantastic Non-Fiction and Get Published by Claire Gillman (Teach Yourself)

Children's Writers' and Artists' Yearbook (A&C Black Publishers)

The Self-Publishing Manual by Dan Poynter (Poynter)

Self-Publishing for Dummies by Jason R. Rich (John Wiley & Sons)

The Complete Guide to Self-Publishing by Tom and Marilyn Ross (Writer's Digest Books)

Aiming at Amazon: The New Business of Self-Publishing by Aaron Shepard (Shepard Publications)

Get Started in Creative Writing by Stephen May (Teach Yourself)

Travel Writing by Don George (Lonely Planet)

Inventing the Truth: Art and Craft of Memoir by Russell Baker (Houghton Miffin)

Writing Your Family History: A Practical Guide by Deborah Cass (Crowood Press)

Writing up Your Family History: A Do-it-yourself Guide by John Titford (Countryside Books)

Publicity, Newsletters and Press Releases by A. Baverstock (Oxford University Press)

On Writing: A Memoir of the Craft by Stephen King (New English Library)

Magazines

UK

The Bookseller

www.thebookseller.com

Writers' Forum

www.writers-forum.com

Writers' News

www.writersnews.co.uk

USA

Writer Magazine

www.writermag.com

Writer's Digest

www.writersdigest.com

Websites

RESEARCH

American Library Association

www.ala.org

British Library

www.bl.uk

+44 (0)843 2081144

British Library Newspapers

+44 (0)843 2081144

Questia (online subscription library specializing in humanities and social sciences)

www.questia.com

ONLINE RESOURCES

Gorkana (UK & US)

www.gorkana.com

News4Media

www.news4media.com

▶ **Journalist alert sites**

Response Source

www.responsesource.com

Craigslist

www.craigslist.org

Sourcewire

www.sourcewire.com

ProfNet

www.profnet.prnewswire.com

AskCharity

www.askcharity.org.uk

TravMedia

www.travmedia.com

Food4Media

www.food4media.com

Health4Media

www.health4media.com

▶ **Blogging**

www.wordpress.com

www.liveJournal.com

www.blogger.com

www.typepad.com

Handbook for Bloggers and Cyber-Dissidents from www.reporterswithoutborders.com

▶ **Ebooks**

Adobe Acrobat

http://get.adobe.com/uk/reader/

Directory of e-publishers

www.ebookcrossroads.com/epublishers.html

e-junkie (ebook publisher)

www.e-junkie.com

Paypal (processes online payments)

www.paypal.com

Amazon

(Allows you to create a store front that accepts orders and processes credit card transactions)

http://webstore.amazon.com/

Google Checkout (processes online payments)

http://checkout.google.com/sell

Kagi (processes online payments)

www.kagi.com

▶ **Self-publishing**

www.greenbay.co.uk/advice

▶ Writing for business

Forum of Private Businesses

www.fpb.org

British Chambers of Commerce

www.britishchambers.org.uk

▶ Radio and television

www.iTunes.com

www.audacity.com

www.apple.com/ilife

www.bbc.co.uk/writersroom

www.simplyscripts.com

▶ Ghost-writing

International Association of Professional Ghostwriters

www.iapgw.org

Association of Ghostwriters (USA)

www. associationofghostwriters.org

Shannon Kyle

www.shannonkyle.co.uk

▶ Professional help for writers

National Council for the Training of Journalists

www.nctj.com

The Writers' Workshop

www.writersworkshop.co.uk

GoldDust (writers mentoring service)

www.gold-dust.org.uk

Jerwood Foundation

www. jerwoodcharitablefoundation.org

The Arts Council England

www.artscouncil.org.uk

American Inland Revenue Service (IRS)

www.irs.gov/individuals/ article/0,,id=222209,00.html

Claire Gillman

www.clairegillman.com

International Federation of Journalists

www.ifj.org

American Press Association

www. americanpressassociation.com

Press Association (UK)

www.pressassociation.com

National Writers' Union (USA)

www.nwu.org

Society of Authors

www.societyofauthors.net

National Union of Journalists

www.nuj.org.uk

For freelance members in London

www.londonfreelance.org.uk

Online News Association (American digital journalism)

www.journalists.org

Authors' Licensing and Collecting Society (ALCS)

(Passes on photocopying and other fees to writers of magazine articles and books)

www.alcs.co.uk

Public Lending Right (PLR)

(Passes on fees from libraries to authors of books)

www.plr.com

National Writers' Union (USA)

www.nwu.org

The Authors' Guild USA

www.authorsguild.org

The Writers' Guild of Great Britain

www.writersguild.org.uk

Author Network

www.author-network.com

Association of Authors' Representatives (USA)

www.aaronline.org

Association of Authors' Agents (AAA)

www.agentsassoc.co.uk

Journalism UK

www.journalismuk.co.uk

Freelance USA

www.freelance.com

Freelance Daily

www.freelancedaily.net

Journalism Jobs

www.journalismjobs.com

Freelance UK

www.freelanceuk.com

Media UK

www.mediauk.com

Writers' Online

www.writers-online.co.uk

Index